GREEN HEART

H L Schofield

*For all the Queer kids.
Especially the grown up ones*

CONTENTS

Title Page
Dedication

Chapter One	1
Chapter Two	7
Chapter Three	14
Chapter Four	23
Chapter Five	30
Chapter Six	35
Chapter Seven	41
Chapter Eight	52
Chapter Nine	61
Chapter Ten	69
Chapter Eleven	76
Chapter Twelve	85
Chapter Thirteen	102
Chapter Fourteen	106
Chapter Fifteen	109
Chapter Sixteen	113

Chapter Seventeen	124
Chapter Eighteen	127
Chapter Nineteen	133
Chapter Twenty	139
Chapter Twenty-One	151
Chapter Twenty-Two	158
Chapter Twenty-Three	168
Chapter Twenty-Four	176
Acknowledgements	181
About The Author	183

Trigger warning

This book contains references to rape, sexual assult, violence, misogyny and homophobia.

CHAPTER ONE

Rowan Fletcher slipped between the shadows like an eel through ink. She approached the nearest house. Firelight flickered at the windows. Good, someone was still up.

Softly, Rowan tapped her knuckles on the door. It opened at once. The face of a middle-aged woman peered out. Rowan had known this woman, Ellen, a long time. She had once been plump, but the harshness of recent years had hollowed out her face. Now her skin sagged with exhaustion. Worry weighed down her eyes.

"Rowan," she whispered, her eyes darting over the girl's head, scanning the dark for hidden terrors. "What…?"

"Evening, Ellen. Just bringing tonight's delivery."

Rowan raised the basket she was holding and pulled back the cover. She drew a hunk of venison from inside, neatly wrapped in a blood-stained cloth and handed it to Ellen.

The woman stared at her, pale eyes washed out with fear. "We don't have anything to give you in return. The taxes…"

Rowan gave a knowing smile. "That's alright," she

said. "You can pay me back next time."

They went through this charade every night. It was the same for most of the village. Some were able to offer Rowan something in exchange for the meat, such as bread or cheese or fruit, but most could not. They always promised to pay her back later, even though they all knew it would never happen.

Ellen looked reluctant but she took the meat. "Bless you, girl," she said before shutting the door against the night.

Rowan turned and headed for the next house. The people of Locksley might once have been too proud to accept such charity. Not anymore. Pride was a luxury they could no longer afford.

Technically, the forests around Locksley belonged to the King and only those who had his favour, namely nobles, could hunt in them. Rowan objected to this law as a matter of principle. She voiced her objection by hunting the King's game and dividing it up among the villagers. The forests weren't well patrolled and Rowan knew them better than anyone, but it was still risky.

Even when she managed to get out and back without being seen, there wasn't always enough to go around. It was hard just to keep herself fed sometimes, let alone everyone else. Today she had been lucky and had managed to shoot a young buck, big enough to give every house a decent share.

Ever since William d'Aubigny had become the Sheriff of Nottingham four years ago, everyone was struggling. Rowan helped as much as she could, but she was just one girl acting alone. What difference could she really make?

Approaching voices snapped her head up. She

darted into a gap between two houses as a patrol of guards appeared around the corner. Their chain mail gleamed in the light of the torches they carried. Their faces were etched deep with shadow. In their midst, Rowan could make out a tall, black-clad figure. Sir Guy of Gisborne, Lord of Locksley and the Sheriff's favourite.

What was he doing out of his manor? Probably looking for some poor soul to beat up for breaking curfew. Gisborne liked delivering punishment.

Rowan waited until the group was out of sight before she slid out of her hiding place. She turned to move on to the next house. She had plenty more to get through that night.

A hand closed over her arm, tight as a snare, and spun her around.

"What are you doing out here?" a voice said as another hand pulled back the hood of her green cloak, letting loose a long braid of auburn hair. He gripped her chin, twisting her face up to the thin moonlight.

She found herself staring at Sir Guy himself. He must have caught a glimpse of her and doubled back.

He grinned at the sight of her. He was dark-haired and handsome, with a sweeping nose, chiselled chin and piercing blue eyes.

"A girl in boy's clothes. What a novelty." He chuckled as Rowan writhed and twisted in his grip.

"Let go of me!"

"*You* do not talk to me like that. You should know who I am. What's this?"

He snatched the basket from her, peeled back the cloth to see at the deer meat inside. His smile was sharp as starlight.

"So, you're a thief as well as insolent. Don't you

know the punishment for poaching?"

He cast the basket aside, grasped her with both hands and pulled her in close. The hot-leather stink of him choked her.

"I'll tell you what, if you make me happy for a few minutes, I'll forget all about it."

He tried to throw her against the wall. She twisted wildly, panic clawing in her chest. Her spare hand groped in her pocket, closing over something sharp. A broken arrowhead. In one movement she pulled it free and slashed out wildly.

Blood spurted black in the moonlight. Gisborne fell to his knees, clutching his face and howling.

Rowan was already running, flying through the village with her cloak streaking out behind her. She heard Gisborne shrieking for his guards, ordering them after her.

Rowan doubled her speed. She crashed into her cottage in a mess of tangled hair and sawing breath. Her eyes scoured the clutter for what she might need, her hands frenzied in panic. She stuffed what food she had into a leather pack, pulled her bow and quiver over her shoulder, thrust a hunting knife through her belt.

She heard a shout outside and peered through the window. She saw torch-wielding guards striding through the village, pounding on doors, issuing commands, searching for the girl who had maimed Sir Guy. She had to leave *now*.

Swinging her pack onto her back and pulling her hood back over her face, she dropped out the cottage's back window and took off through the village. She kept low, slipping from shadow to shadow.

Soon the woods were ahead of her, a shaggy black

mass against the stars. She felt a surge of triumph. She was almost there.

A shout came from behind her. She looked around and cursed. One of the guards had spotted her. Now they were all running towards her, boots thudding in an echo of her frantic heart.

She sprinted for the forest. Many people feared it, believing it to be the haunt of ghosts and spirits. Even if these men weren't superstitious, the darkness beneath the trees should be enough to keep her hidden.

She ducked into the rustling shadows. When she was sure she was out of the guard's sight, she grabbed a low-hanging branch and heaved herself up, scrambling up the tree as high as she could go. She had used this tree plenty of times for scouting deer. She knew it well enough to find the foot and handholds even in the dark.

She had only just got herself secure in the branches when torchlight came flickering through the trees. Three guards appeared beneath her. Rowan didn't move. She barely breathed. Heart clanging, she watched as the guards cast about with their torches, searching for some sign of their quarry.

She heard their resentful mutterings but was too far away to make out the words. It was clear that they were reluctant to risk getting lost in the night-time forest for the sake of one fugitive. Superstitions aside, there were real dangers in the woods after dark: wolves and bandits. The men seemed to be trying to decide whether these were worse than Gisborne's wrath.

Rowan watched them discuss it, praying to every god she'd ever heard of and a few she'd invented that they wouldn't look up. Finally, the men seemed to decide that continuing the search now was pointless, and turned back to the village to face their master.

Rowan waited until she was sure that they had all gone before she swung herself back down to the forest floor. She couldn't stay here, it was too close to the village. She dared not build a fire and without one she'd have to keep moving. It may be spring, but the night air was still chill. She would walk until dawn and find a tree to sleep in. And then...

She felt a sudden surge of panic. This was her life now. She had wounded a lord, she could never go back to Locksley. She would spend the rest of her days running and hiding and scraping to survive.

She took her head in her hands, leaned against a tree for support. She heaved several deep breaths of the cold night air, relishing the familiar forest smells of damp leaves, rich earth and old wood.

No use fretting now, she told herself. *Just keep moving. Get somewhere safe. One step at a time.*

She hitched her pack higher on her back. She felt the reassuring weight of her bow and quiver, like a parent's hand on her shoulder.

Without looking back, she took off into the heart of the forest.

CHAPTER TWO

Rowan woke with a start, jolted from nightmares of Gisborne lunging for her out of the darkness, his hungry eyes and bruising grip, a vicious smile savouring her fear.

She was momentarily surprised to find herself up a tree, tied to a bough with her belt. Then it all came back to her. The mad dash from the village. Hiding from the guards. Stumbling through the dark until dawn had tinged the sky grey and she couldn't walk any further. Gisborne…

She rubbed a hand across her eyes, trying to push the memories aside. She could tell by the sun's height that it was around midday. She felt stiff and sore and distinctly unrested, but there was no helping that. She dug a hunk of bread out of her pack and chewed it while she stretched and massaged the cricks out of her neck, wondering what to do next.

There seemed to be nothing else but to keep going. She still wasn't far enough away from the village. She needed to get deep into the forest and find somewhere, a hollow or a clearing, where she could set up camp.

She saw herself suddenly, living out the rest of her

life in the forest, eternally alone, eternally afraid.

She shook her head firmly. *Don't be stupid,* she told herself. *It's not like you ever cared much for the company of others. And you know how to survive in the woods. Dad taught you everything. So stop whining and get a move on!*

She untied herself and scrambled down the tree. She joined a deer trail and followed it deeper into the forest.

It was one of those delicious days in late spring, the air sweet as honeysuckle, the sunshine making everything brand new. The trees stood fresh and proud in their first flush of leaves. Bluebells were pushing their delicate heads towards the sun. The air was bright with birdsong and hope.

Despite the terrors of the previous night, Rowan felt her spirits lifting. Here at least, she could belong. The forest had fed her for most of her life. It had given her comfort when she needed it most. It had given her somewhere to hide when life under Gisborne's heel had become too much. Now, it would keep her safe.

As she walked, she found herself scanning her surroundings, reading the forest as her father had taught her. She saw fox scat, boar tracks, the scrapings in the earth where a badger had dug for worms. Here, a thrush had smashed a snail open against a protruding root, the shards of shell still visible. Here, a stag had stopped to scrape the velvet from his antlers on a low-lying branch, leaving deep grooves in the bark.

A sound behind her. The short, sharp snap of a twig breaking underfoot. She spun around, knife drawn, her spare hand reaching for her bow. She froze, every sense straining for the source of the noise. There, through the trees. A flash of something pale. The swish of a cloak.

She needed to get off the trail. She darted behind the nearest tree, her back against the wood, trying to quiet her frantic breathing. No chance of climbing to safety this time, the tree was straight and narrow, its branches not starting until more than twice her height up. No time to find a better hiding place either, the approaching figure was almost on her.

Whoever they were, they were making no attempt at stealth. She could hear the crackle of their footsteps through the leaf litter, the huff of their breath. If they came any closer, they would see her. She would have to take them by surprise and hope that she could overpower them.

She took a deep breath. Then she exploded out from behind the tree, pouncing on the stranger and taking them to the ground. She heard them yelp in surprise.

She pinned them with her knees, one hand clamped their mouth shut before they could cry out again. She pressed her knifepoint against their neck to stop them struggling. A pair of pale eyes peered up at her, wide with surprise. She recognised them at once.

"Mathew!" she gasped. She withdrew her hand from his mouth, gazing at him in shock. "What are you doing here?"

He blinked up at her. "I came to find you," he said reproachfully. "Why, is this a bad time?"

Rowan gave a sigh, her limbs going soft with the escaping tension. She rolled off him and Mathew sat up, brushing dirt and leaves from his clothes.

He was eighteen, the same age as Rowan, but he had a spindly, underfed look that made him seem younger. He had been born with almost no colour. His skin was pale. His hair, eyebrows and eyelashes were swan-feather white. His eyes were the washed-out grey of winter skies.

Mathew was a gentle soul, serious and sombre, with a keen interest in the world around him. But all of his life, people had whispered of devils and bad omens whenever they saw him. Some had even called him a changeling, a fae in disguise as a human child. When they were younger, Rowan had bloodied several of the village boys' noses for calling Mathew a freak and pelting him with stones.

Rowan had always felt something of an outsider herself, being a girl who had never quite fitted into what that meant. As a result, the two had become friends.

Mathew's parents were the village millers. They had done what they could for their son, but he had always been a sickly child. It seemed a miracle that he had survived this long. What he was doing so far out in the woods, Rowan had no idea. How he had even got this far without getting lost was a mystery.

"Why did you come to find me?" she asked, getting to her feet and helping Mathew up with her.

"Gisborne," he replied. "He's looking for you. I saw him in the village this morning with half his face bandaged up. He's got his men searching every building in Locksley, and more scouting the forest. I had to come and make sure you were alright. Don't worry," he added when he saw her face, "no one saw me."

"How did you find me?"

Mathew shrugged. "I just followed the route we walk together," he said. "I figured you'd come this way because barely anyone else uses this trail."

Rowan was surprised he could remember the route so well. Mathew's eyesight was very poor and he sometimes struggled to find his way around the forest. She was also dismayed to realise that he was right, without thinking she had been keeping to her own favourite trails. She would need to be less predictable if she wanted to survive past her first week on the run.

"I'm sorry, Mathew, but you've got to go. If you can find me, so can Gisborne. It's not safe for you here."

"I brought food," Mathew said, holding up a cloth bundle as if that answered everything. "And I thought I could keep watch while you got some rest. No offence, but you look terrible."

"Thanks," Rowan muttered.

She knew he wasn't wrong. She had been walking most of the afternoon and couldn't deny that last night's escape and the lack of sleep were starting to take their toll. It would be good to relax for a bit knowing there another person listening for trouble. It would also be good to share a meal with her best friend as if nothing had changed.

"Alright," she relented. "Let's get off the path and find somewhere we can settle."

They pushed their way through the undergrowth, coming at last to a small clearing. Mathew sat down and began unwrapping his bundle. Rowan threw down her pack, bow and quiver, flexing her aching shoulders.

Mathew divided the bread and cheese between the two of them. There wasn't much. Food was scarce these days.

They chewed in companionable silence. Rowan watched a pair of woodpeckers making a nest in a hollow of a tree, flying in and out with beaks full of twigs and moss.

"Gisborne's saying you attacked him for no reason,"

Mathew said eventually, his eyes downcast, his tone cautious, "but I'm sure that's not true." He looked up at her, his eyes huge. "You don't have to tell me," he said gently. "But if you want to, you can."

Rowan didn't want to, not really. But she felt as if she owed Mathew the truth after he had come all this way and shared his food.

She told him everything, what Gisborne had done, what he said, her desperate escape. It was hard, but as she said the words, she felt lighter. Mathew stared at her, his pale eyes seeming to go right through her, his face soft with sorrow.

"I'm sorry," he said, laying a hand on her shoulder.

He seemed unsure of what else to say, of how much comfort to offer, reluctant perhaps to dent her pride. Rowan nodded to show the gesture was appreciated. She didn't trust herself to say more.

"If it helps, I think you tore his eye out."

"Good," said Rowan, the savagery in her voice surprising her. "He deserved worse. If he comes near me again, I'll kill him."

She felt taken aback by her words. She meant them, and yet... Killing a human wasn't the same as killing a rabbit or a deer. She remembered Gisborne's screams as he clutched at his face, the blood bubbling between his fingers. She didn't regret what she'd done but still, those grating cries haunted her.

Rowan finished her food and straightened up. "Come on," she said, turning to Mathew. "We should…"

She stopped when she saw his expression. He was staring at something behind her, his face fixated in terror. Spinning around, Rowan saw a figure step out of the trees as if materialising from leaves and bark.

Their clothes were shades of brown and green, better to blend in with the forest. A scarf covered the lower part of their face. They had a loaded bow aimed at Rowan's chest.

Rowan heard Mathew gasp beside her as two more figures appeared, silent as smoke, surrounding them in a circle of bristling arrows and scowls.

"I'm afraid you won't be leaving just yet," the first figure said. Rowan could hear the hidden smile behind the words. "We need to get better acquainted first."

CHAPTER THREE

Rowan and Mathew sat, bound hand and foot, watching the outlaws devour the last of Rowan's supplies. They ate so ferociously that it was clear they hadn't had a decent meal in some time.

They had removed their scarves and it was now possible to make out their faces. Two girls around Rowan's age, and a boy a little younger. It seemed that one of the girls was the leader. She was taller and broader than any woman Rowan had ever seen, with a wild tangle of russet hair. The other two deferred to her in all things, whether out of fear or respect Rowan couldn't tell.

"What do you think they'll do to us?" Mathew whispered. He looked more boyish than ever in his terror, his face so white it was almost translucent.

The russet-haired girl looked up at his question. "Don't worry, little boy," she said. "We only kill nobles, which you're obviously not. We'll just drop you by the road somewhere, maybe knock you about a bit so you don't remember our faces. Someone will come along and find you."

Mathew looked slightly if not completely reassured, but Rowan's heart gave a clutch of fear. "You can't," she said, the sharpness in her voice betraying her panic. "I'm wanted by the law. Sir Guy of Gisborne has got men all over the forest looking for me. If you leave me bound or unconscious somewhere, you're as good as handing me to him."

The russet-haired girl cocked her head. "Really? What did you do?"

Rowan couldn't face telling the whole story again. "Let's just say I ruined Gisborne's pretty face for him."

The girl chuckled darkly, the others joining in. Even outside Locksley, Gisborne was clearly unpopular. Rowan felt a speck of hope. If she could build a rapport with these outlaws, she might be able to persuade them to let her and Mathew go.

"What about you? What was your crime?"

The big girl shrugged. "Refusing to starve," she said bluntly. "Thievery, poaching, not paying taxes… You name it, we've done it."

"Poaching?" Mathew said, eying their ragged, hungry appearance. "You mean you hunt?"

The other girl, slender and dark-haired, laughed. "It was more like attempted poaching. Alan tried to kill a deer but he's a terrible shot. Anyway, some of the Sheriff's men saw and so we had to run."

The boy glared over at the young woman. "Shut *up*, Willow."

"Rowan can hunt," Mathew piped up. "She's the best shot in the whole of Locksley. She could teach you, then you won't have to rely on robbing travellers for food."

The russet-haired girl looked at Rowan curiously. "Best shot in Locksley. That so?"

Rowan fought the urge to glare at Mathew, keeping her face smooth and impassive. "Give me back my bow and I'll show you."

The big girl laughed. "You really think I'm that stupid?"

Rowan swallowed the witty retort that sprung to her lips. She gazed longingly at her bow and quiver, stacked neatly with her pack and knife just a few feet away. It might as well have been a thousand.

"She can fight too," Mathew said. "Better than any of the boys in the village. Her father was a soldier; he taught her how."

Rowan dearly wanted to tell Mathew to shut up, but there was a gleam in his eyes that said he was having one of his ideas and there was no use stopping him. "How about a wager? Rowan fights the strongest amongst you and if she wins, you let her stay."

Rowan scowled at Mathew in indignation, but the big girl laughed and nodded. "Alright, little boy, you're on."

She got to her feet. The other girl, Willow, got up too, her face concerned. "June, this is foolish. We don't know them; we can't trust them."

June waved away her concerns as if they were flies. "If I win, we won't have to."

She stood grinning at Rowan, clearly in no doubt how this would go. Privately, Rowan agreed. She did know how to fight, but the other girl was twice as broad as she was and nearly half again as tall. Her hands looked strong enough to snap Rowan in two.

At a gesture from June, Willow cut Rowan free. She then planted herself over Rowan's weapons, her knife still drawn, face sharp with mistrust.

Rowan got to her feet, shaking the cramp from her limbs. Somehow, even standing didn't make June seem any less massive. The other girl stood across from her, smiling widely.

"Let's say no weapons," she said, eyeing Rowan's scrawny frame as if searching for the weakest point. "And the first person to yield or be rendered unable to continue loses, agreed?"

Rowan jerked a nod. *If I survive this, Mathew, I am going to kill you.*

There was no countdown, no call for a start. June just came at her, fists swinging. Rowan managed to duck the first punch, but the second caught her a glancing blow across the jaw. She staggered backwards, feeling as if her head had been split open. She rubbed her jaw to check it wasn't broken. She could hear June and the other outlaws laughing.

Shaking the clanging from her skull, she straightened up and faced the other girl again. June came at her, jabbing for her face and gut. Rowan dodged, dropped in low and slammed a kick into the other girl's knee. The leg buckled. June stumbled, almost went down, bellowing like a bull.

Rowan scooted out of the way and came at June from behind, trying to get her in a chokehold. June gave a roar, grabbed hold of Rowan's tunic and threw her over her head as easily as if she were a sack of feathers.

Rowan hit the forest floor with a whumpf of escaping air. She rolled aside before June's boot could stamp down on her ribs. She scrambled to her feet. A nearby tree gave her a sudden burst of inspiration.

She ran for it, with June thundering after her. She grabbed the lowest branch and swung herself up, bringing June up short in surprise. Rowan dived at her, wrapping her arms and legs around the tall girl's neck and bearing her to the ground. She tightened the hold as much as she could, heard June's throat rasp as she struggled for breath.

"Do you yield?" Rowan panted.

In response, June got an elbow between their bodies, forcing Rowan away with incredible strength. Rowan rolled, came up in a crouch, saw June barrelling towards her with murder in her eyes.

Looking around she saw that Willow had moved with the fight and no longer stood over her weapons. She dived for them, out of June's path. She rolled as June turned, grabbed her bow and came upon one knee, arrow nocked and aimed at June's face.

June came to a halt, her chest heaving. "You cheated," she growled. "We agreed no weapons."

Rowan grinned up at her. "I thought that the whole point of being an outlaw was that you didn't have to follow the rules."

For a moment, June's scowl deepened. Then it broke into a smile and she let out a bark of raucous laughter.

"So it is," she said. She turned to Willow and Alan, both slack-jawed with shock, and gestured at Mathew. "Let him go."

They obeyed at once. Rowan let her bow drop, straightening to her feet. June was eyeing the weapon.

"Are you as good with that thing as he says you are?"

In response, Rowan bent over her pack, scooping up the heel of bread that was all that remained of her rations. She tossed it to Mathew with a grin. "Care to do the honours?"

Mathew beamed back. Then, just as they'd practiced many times before, he tossed the bread into the air as high as he could. In one movement, Rowan raised the bow, drew back the string and let fly. The arrow stuck the bread mid-flight and they both fell back to earth with a soft thump.

June raised her eyebrows. "Impressive."

She stuck out her hand. "My name's June Littlewood," she said. "And I always keep my word. There's a place for you here if you want it."

Rowan raised a wry eyebrow. "*Little*wood?"

June grinned and shrugged. "We can't help the names we're given. And you? Rowan what?"

"Fletcher." Rowan took June's hand and shook it, trying not to wince at how her fingers were nearly crushed in the strong girl's grip. She crooked a smile at June. "And it is my pleasure to accept your gracious offer."

❊ ❊ ❊

Later, when the darkness was drawing in and the outlaws had found a place to camp, Rowan took Mathew aside.

"You need to get back to Locksley," she said, keeping her voice low so the others wouldn't hear, "before you're missed. I really appreciate all you've done for me today, even if I'd rather you came up with a way that didn't get me hit so much. But it's not safe for you here."

Mathew shook his head. His eyes were bright and eager. "No, I'm staying," he said. "This could be the opportunity we need."

Rowan frowned at him. "What do you mean, 'we'? *You're* not an outlaw."

"I've assisted one. That's basically the same thing."

"Mathew…"

"No, just listen. This is it, don't you see? This is our chance to make a difference."

"What do you mean? Make a difference how?"

"By fighting back!" His voice was clear and bright, he made no attempt to muffle his words. The others had been looking over in interest and now gathered around to listen.

"Don't you see? We can do more than just steal food from poor travellers. All sorts of people pass through the forest on their way to Nottingham. Wealthy lords, the Sheriff's tax collectors. You can rob them, give the money back to the people, where it belongs."

"It wouldn't work," Rowan said. "Those people always travel with an armed guard. We'd never even get close."

"I've seen you fight," Mathew said. "You can teach us."

"I've fought *boys*, Mathew. These will be grown men, trained soldiers, with armour and *swords*. We've got wooden bows and fire-hardened arrows. How do you expect us to…?"

"We can get weapons," Mathew said dismissively. "Or make them. You've been able to fletch arrows since you were five, you told me so."

"This isn't a game, little boy," June said, her voice a rumbling growl. "You'd be asking us to risk our lives. And for what?"

"For a chance to help the loved ones you left behind and bloody the Sheriff's nose at the same time!" Mathew cried. His eyes were feverish now. "How is that not worth fighting for?"

He turned to Rowan. "Surely you understand this. You risked your life every day, hunting the King's deer to feed the people of Locksley. If you'd been caught, they would have hung you, but you did it anyway."

Willow looked at Rowan, surprised. "That was you? My aunt's from Locksley. She told us someone was doing that. I never thought…" She trailed off, looking at Rowan with something like respect for the first time.

Rowan squirmed uncomfortably. "That was different. I didn't do it to be a hero. I just wanted to get back at the Sheriff and his lords for what they'd done to my family."

"Exactly!" Mathew exclaimed. "That's what I'm suggesting. Defying the Sheriff and feeding people at the same time. What could be better?"

Rowan stared into his fierce, excited face. She thought of Gisborne with his grasping eyes, throwing her against the wall as if she were nothing. She thought of her father, his legs jerking as the rope cut into his neck. She thought of her mother, so frail a whisper could have blown her away. She remembered her mum's voice, murmuring to Rowan to stay alive, to stay strong, as her own pulse slowly trickled away.

She felt all the swirling anger and grief harden into something sharp and cold. Purpose.

"Alright," she said, her voice low. "I'm in. I'll teach anyone who wants to fight and shoot as best I can. And then… yes, I say we go with Mathew's plan. We take back what's been stolen and give it to the people it belongs to."

Alan agreed at once, his face flushed and excited as a small boy agreeing to a game of soldiers. Willow did too, after some consideration, glancing at Alan in concern. Only June took her time, grinding the problem between her teeth before finally relenting.

"Alright," she grumbled. "We'll try it."

She glared around at them. "But if I die because of this, I am seriously going to haunt every single one of you."

CHAPTER FOUR

"Try again," Rowan said with a suppressed sigh as June's shot fell short once more. "You need to tighten your grip, otherwise you're not going to get the power."

June eyed the slender piece of wood in her huge hands dubiously as if she feared breaking it. "I much prefer a weapon you can bash someone with," she muttered as she went to retrieve the arrows.

Rowan turned to the others. They were in a clearing not far from camp, and Rowan had used charcoal to draw up targets for each of them on a row of silver birch trees.

They had been practising for weeks, and it was beginning to show. At the tree beside June's, Willow nocked, drew and loosed an arrow all in one breath, hitting her tree just a little off from the central target. Rowan smiled at her, impressed. Willow was easily the best shot after Rowan, and she had picked the skill up with surprising speed.

At the next tree along, her brother drew back his bow. Alan was enthusiastic but erratic, the base of his tree littered with arrows that had missed their mark.

As Rowan watched, he let fly and his arrow leapt away, missing his tree by a whisker.

"Close," Rowan said, stepping forwards to correct his stance and grip. "Remember the arrow is going to dip slightly as it flies, so it's good to aim a little higher than the target itself."

She stepped along the line again until she came to Mathew's tree. Of all of them, her best friend had struggled the most. His poor eyesight made aiming difficult, but he had persisted with a clench-jawed determination. As she approached, Rowan could see that he hadn't hit the target once this session. The frustration was building in his eyes, burning his face red.

"Just breathe," Rowan said gently as she stood beside him. "Nock the arrow and take a breath. Drawback and take another before you loose. Slow your heartbeat down, or you'll only make your aim worse."

Mathew looked at her, on the verge of tears. "I'll never be good enough," he said mournfully. "I shouldn't come out on missions. I'll just be a burden, put you all in danger."

Rowan laughed softly. "Are you kidding? I wouldn't even be here if it wasn't for you. You're the brains of the whole operation, we'd be lost without you. Now."

She took Mathew's hands in hers, raised them up and positioned them on his bow, just like her father used to do for her. "Take a breath, relax your shoulders and try again."

Mathew did as she said, taking a deep breath and sighing it out through his teeth. He closed his eyes for a moment. When he opened them, he drew back the arrow and let fly. It thudded into the trunk of his tree, a good hands length from where Rowan had drawn the target but still, it was the first time he'd struck wood all day.

"Excellent!" Rowan cried, clapping him on the shoulder. "As long as you can hit it reliably at ten paces, you'll be fine."

"Yeah," Alan called over, his eyes bright with mischief. "After all, those lords and tax collectors don't need to know that there's only one decent shot among us." He flashed a cheeky smile at Willow and added, "my sister doesn't count."

Willow reached over to thump Alan on the arm and he danced away, laughing. Mathew joined in the laughter, his eyes shining, all thought of tears forgotten. Rowan felt her heart melt at the sight of it.

She and Mathew had been with the outlaws for several weeks now, and he had surprised her with how well he had adapted to their wild, wandering life. She had learned a lot about her best friend in recent weeks and indeed about all the outlaws.

She learned that Willow, who had been taught herb lore by her mother, could identify every plant in the forest and name all its properties and uses.

She learned that Alan had the purest, sweetest singing voice she had ever heard. He regaled them around the fire every night with ballads of heroes and warriors and great adventures of old.

She learned that June could fell a tree with one swing of her axe, that her laugh was as warm and catching as wildfire.

"Sometimes, when everyone acts like you are a certain way, you become like that so they can't use it against you," June had told Rowan about a week after they first met, when they were out hunting together. "People see my size and they think I'm unnatural, that it's wrong for a woman to be so big. They assume I must be brutish, stupid, cruel..." She looked away, sudden pain creasing her broad face. "Like my father."

June's mother died when she was small. She ran away from her father when she was fifteen. He was even bigger than she was, a drunk, easy with his fists. She fled his rages and set herself up in the same village as Alan and Willow. She lived in a small tumbledown shack on the village's edge and done whatever jobs her size and strength lent themselves to.

But it had barely been enough to keep herself fed, so she refused to pay the outlandish taxes the Sheriff demanded. When the guards came for her, June had been chopping wood outside her house. She managed to injure two of them before she got away and had been living in the forest ever since.

Rowan found out quickly that Willow and Alan were half-brother and sister. Neither of them knew their fathers; their mother wouldn't talk about them. They didn't look much alike. Willow was tall and slim with long, dark hair and light brown skin. Alan was paler with a short, stocky build, his hair a curly chestnut. They shared only their hazel eyes and long straight noses.

The two of them had known June before they were outlawed. She had helped to fix the thatch of their cottage a few seasons ago. Willow and Alan's mother had taken pity on the large girl. From then on, she had done what she could to make sure June got enough food, gave her herbs when she was ill and mended her clothes. The three youngsters had grown close. After June had become outlawed, Willow and Alan still tried to keep in touch with her as much as they could, seeking her out whenever they were in the woods. Then, when they were caught poaching, they went to join her.

Everyone quickly found their own role in the group. Alan, who had been apprenticed to a tanner before becoming outlawed, made quivers and bow casings from the skins of animals Rowan caught. Willow gathered herbs to heal their injuries, along with mushrooms, nuts, berries and edible leaves to bulk out their meals. June chopped and gathered firewood and built the shelters when they moved camp. Rowan hunted.

Mathew's role was quite different. His bad eyesight made it impossible to hunt or gather like the others. He became their planner. His mental map of the forest roads meant that he knew good points to set up an ambush. He found places where all five of them could hide and spread out so it seemed like there were more of them. He schemed and plotted and stayed up late coming up with ever more elaborate strategies.

Rowan kept her part of the deal and taught them all to shoot as best she could. She equipped them all with decent bows, for the ones they had already were shoddy at best. Her father had taught her how to make good, strong bows out of the finest yew, threaded with gut skin. She fletched them straight, spruce wood arrows and hardened the tips in the fire, as they had no steel arrowheads.

She also showed them what hand to hand combat techniques her father had taught her from his time as an infantry bowman in the King's army. They used fallen branches in place of swords and grappled on the forest floor. Rowan showed them how to land blows with their fists and feet and anything else they could use.

June, unsurprisingly, proved herself proficient. Rowan's jaw still liked to remind her not to cross the other girl. The others picked up the skills quickly enough and Rowan was immensely satisfied with their progress in such a short time.

And even though she still woke up from nightmares of Gisborne, even though she started at every snapping twig like a frightened rabbit, Rowan found she was happier than she had been for nearly a year. For the first time, she had a purpose. More than that, she had belonging. She had people she belonged to. And for the moment, that was enough.

Soon there wasn't enough light left to aim properly, so they packed up and headed back to camp. Overall, it had been one of their better practice sessions, and Rowan was impressed with everyone's improvement.

They spit-roasted a pair of wood pigeons Rowan had shot earlier and ate in companionable silence, everyone too tired and sore from the day's excursions to talk much.

Rowan sat fletching arrows by firelight, an activity so familiar she could do it with her eyes closed. She looked around at the four other faces, bathed in golden glow and sharp shadow. They were no longer a motley band of teenage miscreants, thrown together by circumstance. They were a team now, a unit, an army. Soon, they would be ready to commence with Mathews plan.

Fear clawed her lungs at the thought. If one of them got hurt or even killed, it would be on her. She was the one who had agreed to Mathew's idea, who had put the weapons in their hands, taught them to fight. It would be her leading them into danger. If something happened to them, any of them, how would she forgive herself?

Gisborne's hungry eyes loomed out of the darkness

beyond the fire. She felt his grip crush her wrist, smelt the hot leather stink of his body against hers. She shook herself off, hardened her heart. Anything that made that bastard pay had to be worth it.

CHAPTER FIVE

"I'll ask you again," Sir Guy of Gisborne said, wiping his knuckles on a bloody rag. "Where is she?"

The bound man coughed and retched, blood drooling from his mangled lips. "I told you already," he rasped. "The last I saw her was that night a few weeks back when she came to our house."

"Oh really? And why was she there?"

The man squirmed in his bonds. "I don't know. My wife answered the door. I don't know what they talked about."

He was lying, Gisborne could tell. The lord let a wolfish smile creep up his face. "Well, maybe it's your wife I should be speaking to."

The old man stared up at him, bruised eyes round and pleading. "No, please! She knows no more about this than I do, I swear!"

Gisborne gave a sigh that was more of a snarl. In truth, he had no interest in dowdy peasant housewives, and if she proved as stubborn as her husband, he'd only be wasting his time. In his weeks of interrogating the villagers, searching for the girl who had maimed him, all he had got was her name, Rowan Fletcher. Even then, he sensed they had only told him it because the girl had vanished, melting into the forest like mist under the morning sun.

She had lived alone as far as he could tell. No family or friends to speak of except for some miller's son. The boy had, conveniently enough, also disappeared.

"Gone to visit a relative in a distant village" was all he could get out of the millers when he went looking. He had considered having them arrested and publicly executed in the hope of luring the pair out but knew it wouldn't be prudent. The whole village relied on the mill for flour, including him, and there was no one else who could work the blasted thing.

He had been left with nothing to do but offer dire threats and well-placed bruises. If their son or the girl made contact, the millers were to report to him immediately. But even as he had strode away, boiling over with frustration, he had known they wouldn't comply.

That was the strangest thing. In any other village, a young woman living alone, refusing to marry and strutting around in man's clothes, would attract all the wrong kinds of attention. The villagers should have been desperate to give her up. Instead, they seemed strangely loyal towards her, almost protective. Why? What had she been doing that night he caught her?

Pain broke through his thoughts, spiking high behind his injured eye. He rubbed at it angrily. The bandages had come off, replaced with a leather patch. Still, the wound gnawed at his skull, stealing his sleep and blighting his days. When he got hold of the girl who had done this to him...

Knowing that he would get no more out of the

peasant, he snapped at his men to get the wretch out of here. As Gisborne strode up from the cool dark of the cellar into the airy brightness of the manor, the sunlight stabbed into his skull, lighting up his scar in lines of fire.

He snarled at a passing maid to fetch him wine. She bobbed a curtsy, eyes downcast, and scurried off. He caught a flash of the bruises at her wrists, dark against pale skin. The outlines of grasping fingers were clearly visible. Despite the pain chewing through his head, Gisborne found himself smiling at the memory.

He collapsed into the nearest chair, gulping down the wine the serving girl brought him and sending her off for more. He leaned back, closed his eyes. He had just managed to calm the pain in his head to a bearable throb when a slight cough roused him. He looked up to see a boy dressed in the uniform of a castle servant standing over him, straight-backed with his hands folded behind him.

"What are you doing here?"

"M-my apologies, my lord," the lad said with a nervous bow. "One of your servants let me in. I have a message for you, sir."

Sir Guy sighed, waved a languid hand. "Out with it then."

The boy cleared his throat. "The Sheriff orders you to report to Nottingham at once, sir."

Gisborne bristled at the word "orders". What was he, a dog for d'Aubigny to kick around? The slimy little man would never have gotten where he was without Gisborne there to do his dirty work.

"The next council is in three days," Gisborne replied, leaning back once more. "Whatever the Sheriff has to tell me can wait until then."

The boy swallowed noisily. "I beg your pardon, sir,

but this can't wait. His Lordship was very clear on that. It's a matter of urgency, he says."

Gisborne frowned at the messenger. "Why? What's happened?"

"A tax collectors' wagon was attacked by outlaws this morning, sir, as it travelled through the forest to Nottingham."

Gisborne gave a huff of frustration. "That's hardly news, boy! It happens all the time. They never get much."

"This time they did, sir. They were organised, cunning, and they made off with the whole lot. What's more, this is the third such attack this week. Tax convoys, visiting nobility, travelling abbots, all are arriving at Nottingham stripped of their valuables, all by the same gang. They're led by a masked man in a green hood."

Despite everything, the boy's eyes shone, his voice almost reverent as he continued. "They say his skills with the bow are unmatched, almost uncanny. That his strength and speed are beyond human comprehension. That his fighting-prowess is unbeat—"

The boy's words choked off as Gisborne stood up, towering over him.

"Have them prepare my horse." Gisborne's voice was a deadly rumble in his throat. "I ride for Nottingham at once. Go, now!"

The boy did not need telling twice. He scrambled away like a whipped puppy, vanishing out into the sunlight beyond the manor.

Gisborne crossed the room to where he'd left his sword propped against the wall, strapping it to his belt with sharp vicious movements.

So, some flea-bitten bandit or upstart peasant had decided to play hero, had he? Well, they would soon make him regret that. Gisborne and the Sheriff would crush this hooded champion like the weevil he was, ungodly powers or not.

His scar was aching again, pulsing in time with each movement. He massaged it with one hand as he headed into the courtyard, thinking. The girl could wait. His personal vengeance wasn't as important as what he and the Sheriff had built here, the power they needed tax money to maintain. Once they had rid themselves of this troublesome thief, he would hunt down the girl and see them both hang.

He had a sudden image of the girl's eyes, emerald green and glittering with defiance. Her auburn hair flying as she fought in his grip, her teeth gleaming in a snarl of fury.

He allowed himself a grin as he mounted his horse and kicked it towards Nottingham. Oh yes. She would look *very* well in a noose.

CHAPTER SIX

Rowan peered around the tree trunk at the approaching wagon and ducked back before she was spotted. It was more heavily guarded than the other convoys they'd attacked, a squat, trundling cart laden with the taxes of the nearby villages. It was rumbling along the North Road towards town, accompanied by four armoured guards. No matter, it normally only took a show of loaded bows to get them to hand over their loot. Particularly if you were clever about it.

Rowan adjusted the scarf across her mouth and nose, checked the leather mask Alan had made for her was secure over her eyes. The last thing she needed was a description of her getting back to Gisborne.

She pulled her hood further over her braided hair. She had cut the hood from her cloak and sewn it on to her tunic, so she would never be without it. She had used lichen to dye her tunic a mix of browns and greens, allowing her to better blend in with the forest.

Rowan waited, listening to the rumbling of the cart's wheels until she was certain it was within range. Taking a deep breath, she spun from behind the tree, loosing an arrow as she did so. She heard the thunk as it found the wood of the wagon, the cries of men and startled whinnies of horses.

Darting out from the other side of the tree, she fired a second time. Alan and Willow, hidden in the undergrowth on either side of the road, took this as their queue to loose their own arrows.

The convoy came to a stop, the horses shying and skittish. The men stared around them with drawn swords, certain that they must be surrounded by bloodthirsty bandits but unable to see them.

Rowan nocked another arrow to her bow and stepped into the road. The driver's eyes widened in fear when he saw her.

Before he could do anything else, Mathew and June had stepped across the road behind the wagon. June hefted her axe and scowled above the scarf covering the lower half of her face. Mathew raised his drawn bow, a hood covering his ghost-white hair.

"Good afternoon, gentlemen," Rowan called out. "If you would be so good as to hand over your cargo, we'll be taking it from here."

One of the guards stepped forwards, scowling. His sword was still drawn but he dared not do anything with it while there were an unknown number of arrows fixed on him.

Rowan switched her aim to the young man, pulling him up short. She was surprised to see that she recognised him. It was Colm. He was a lad from her village, one of the brutes she'd often had to drive away from Mathew.

"What kind of man hides his face?" Colm sneered. "Why don't you show yourself, coward?"

"What kind of man preys on the weak?" Rowan said coolly. "What kind of man takes from people with nothing left to give?"

The young man spluttered, choking on his own bluster. It was unexpected, seeing a boy she knew in guard's armour, but not surprising. Colm had always been a bully and with few opportunities elsewhere, plenty of young men were being drawn into the Sheriff's personal army.

At that moment, one of the other men lunged for Mathew. Caught off-guard, he had no time to respond. Rowan managed to loose her arrow into the man's shoulder just before his sword could reach Mathew's throat. The guardsman fell to his knees, howling. June silenced him with a blow to the head.

Colm seized his opportunity and dived for Rowan, sword swinging and hungry for blood. Rowan caught the strike on her bow, then whacked her weapon down into the young man's knees, taking out his legs. He hit the road with a groan. A kick to the head ensured he stayed there.

The cart driver had taken advantage of the chaos and whipped his horses to charge forward. Rowan dived aside before the cart could crush her. It rattled past her, racing for Nottingham and salvation.

But Willow and Alan had not forgotten their job. They leapt out of the forest, loosing arrows into the cart. The horses reared at their sudden appearance, whinnying in fright and bringing the cart to an abrupt halt once again.

Rowan swung herself up next to the driver. He stared at her with boggling eyes, gasping in terror when she pressed her hunting knife to his stomach.

"Now then," Rowan said in her sweetest voice.

"Let's try this again…"

* * *

The evening air smelt of dust and spent sunshine. The fading light was as sweet and golden as apple cider.

Rowan stood just within the treeline around Locksley. She watched people going about their business, emerging from their houses or returning home and marvelling at the small bags of coins they found on their doorsteps. She saw people she had known for years, Ellen, Mathew's parents and a dozen others exclaiming in delight, breaking into laughter or joyful tears at the sight of the gleaming coins, at the hunger-free days it would entail.

Rowan felt a smile tug at the edges of her mouth, a warmth brewing in her belly. They had done countless other "coin drops" as they called them all over Nottinghamshire in the last few months, but she never got tired of it.

As Rowan turned to head back into the depths of the forest, she caught a snatch of sound on the evening breeze.

"The Green Hood," it called. "Wanted for crimes of thievery and murder…"

Curious, Rowan crept around the side of the house, keeping close to the wooden wall.

At the centre of the village square, a town crier stood, a pompous looking little man in elaborate finery, calling out in a clear, carrying voice to a small, unimpressed crowd.

"A reward of fifty pounds is on offer for any information leading to capture. Be warned, this individual is extremely dangerous and not to be approached…"

Shaking her head in disgust, Rowan turned away. Murder? Honestly, she'd never killed anyone! Sighing, she strode away into the woods.

She didn't know where the name "Green Hood" had come from. Certainly not from her. Rumour had become legend, almost overnight. Some said the Green Hood was six foot tall and built like a bear. Others that he had strange, supernatural powers. Still more thought him some kind of forest spirit, the Green Man of the woods.

The only thing everyone seemed to agree on about the Green Hood was that he was a man. Though Rowan was frustrated by this, she had to admit that it helped to conceal her identity. It was lucky in a way that she was fairly tall, her shoulders and arms well-muscled from years of using the bow; so she let assumptions work in her favour for once. Sometimes she even found it fun to be seen in a new way, though it was a surprising and slippery feeling, full of contradictions.

Mathew was thrilled with the name and the stories that came with it. "A faceless figure causes more fear than a known one," he said, eyes bright and shining. "And all the lords are afraid right now. They have no idea who this Green Hood is, so it could be anyone. One of their peasants, the man they sat next to at dinner, the servant who brings them wine. It's about time they learned what fear was."

The afternoon was yawning into evening as Rowan slipped back into the shelter of the trees. She stared into the cathedral dome of branches above her, breathing in the forest's deep, green scent. The moon had swelled and shrunk three times since she had joined the outlaws. Summer had ripened from gentle warmth to blazing heat. Three months of training and ambushes and watching tired faces smile again. Three months of close calls and near misses, of bruises and burning muscles and surging adrenaline. Three months of peace beneath the trees and laughter around the campfire. Three months of finally making a difference. Even though there had been times when she had been more scared than at any other time in her life, Rowan could feel herself settling into this way of life.

And yet, something was missing. A stubborn ache in her chest that she had learned to ignore. The smells of honeyed wood and crushed bracken conjuring memories of another summer, another time, a face with curling hair and dark, dark eyes, a face she'd sworn to forget…

Rowan shook her head, stamping down the memories. She couldn't afford to be distracted with what was long gone. She had people counting on her now, Mathew and the others, the people of Locksley, the whole of Nottingham, relied on her. Their expectations already weighed too heavily across her shoulders. No point in adding to her burden.

Rowan gave herself a little shake, like a dog shedding water, then turned back towards camp.

CHAPTER SEVEN

Rowan sped around a corner, her boots skidding for purchase. The thunder of the guard's footsteps snapped at her heels as she pelted up the street beyond. Above her, the castle glowered down from its rocky perch. The crescent moon glared out from behind it, bright and sharp. The run-down dwellings of the town's poor clung to the castle's skirts, the town pouring down the hill and puddling beneath it.

They had avoided the town for as long as they could, with the guarded gates, unfamiliar terrain and lack of decent hiding places. However, the plight of the city's poor had continued to niggle at them until they had no choice but to come and dispense the stolen taxes.

They had got lucky at the gates, blending in with a crowd of traders, but they soon found that what they remembered as occasional guard patrols were now swarms. As they attempted to walk calmly with what felt like targets on their backs, Rowan wondered if it had always been this way.

Her thoughts were cut short when a guard recognised her now infamous disguise, and their patrol instantly gave chase. Rowan and Mathew became separated in the maze of allies and backstreets, the buildings only growing thicker the closer they got to the castle.

Lungs burning, Rowan tore down street after street. The sounds of the guards behind her were growing closer. She couldn't evade them forever. She could already hear them shouting for backup.

She whipped around another corner and saw an open doorway. Without thinking, she darted into it, pressing her back against the wall within. The smell of smoke and hot metal punched her in the nose. It was a blacksmith's shop, still dimly lit by the bloody glow of embers in the forge. The smith in question must have left the door open to let the heat out. She hoped they didn't come back anytime soon.

She heard the guards run past in a clank of armour and huff of breath, too focused on catching up to their quarry to notice the open doorway. She let out her breath.

"Who are you?"

Rowan's head whipped around, heart pulverising itself against her ribs. Through the smoky dimness, she could make out a huge figure approaching her. A big man in a leather apron, with dark skin and broad shoulders. His bare arms were thick with muscle, nicked by countless scars and old burns. A huge hammer was clasped in one colossal fist.

"What are you doing in here? Trying to steal from me, are you?"

Rowan realised with a jolt that she knew that voice. As the man stepped forward, the crimson light of the forge fell across his face. A scowling, furious face. But a familiar one.

"Roderick," she gasped. But before she could say

more, the hammer swung at her and she had to duck away before her brains painted the wall.

"Get out of here," the man boomed. "Go on, get away!"

But Rowan couldn't leave. She could hear the guards outside, not that far away. They had slowed to a walk, and she could hear the faint rumblings of their frustration. If she left now, they would see her.

"Roderick, wait…" she pleaded, but the big man wasn't listening.

"I said go! No one steals from me!"

He swung for her again. She twisted away just in time. The hammer crashed into a row of swords propped against the wall, sending them flying in all directions. The crashing could have woken half the town.

One of the swords hilts tangled up with Rowan's ankles. She fell back, scrabbling away across the dusty floor. Roderick loomed over her, eyes blazing, hammer raised. Left with nothing else, Rowan did the one thing she had sworn she would never do. She reached up and pulled away her disguise.

"Roderick!" she said, gasping for breath, leaving the mask and scarf hanging around her neck and pushing down her hood. "Roderick, it's me."

The big man stilled, recognition spilling across his face. "Rowan? What… how…?"

There was no time to explain. Rowan could hear the guards approaching once more, drawn by the commotion. Rowan surged to her feet, staring about her desperately for somewhere to hide.

Roderick lowered his hammer, glancing from the frantic girl to the sound of the approaching guards. "They after you?"

Rowan nodded; her heart hammering too hard for her to form words. Roderick took her by the shoulder and pushed her to the back of his shop.

"Get in there," he said, shoving her towards a pile of coal in one corner. Rowan shot him a grateful glance before burrowing into the pile. Soon she was submerged up to her eyes, only her nose protruding to allow her to breathe. Roderick pulled a covering over the heap. It was thick and heavy and filled her nose with the stench of burned leather.

She heard him turn and walk back to the entrance of the shop, heard the guards' footsteps stop as they reached it.

"What?" Roderick snapped.

"A fugitive was seen heading this way," one of the guards said. "We were wondering if you had seen anything."

"No."

"We heard you shouting," the other guard said, his voice a scratchy nasal whine. "Bangs, crashes, that sort of thing."

"There was a rat," Roderick said. "I was trying to see it off."

A tense silence followed. Rowan dared not move. Her breath echoed horribly loud beneath the cover. Dust from the coal was scratching her throat. She fought the urge to cough.

"We need to search your premises," the first guard said. "This fugitive is highly dangerous, and it is a matter of great urgency."

Rowan's heart seized up. Every muscle in her body tightened.

Roderick laughed, deep and slow. She heard the

slap of metal on skin as he hoisted the hammer in both hands.

"You are not coming in here," he said with a deep growl. "This is my property and the likes of you aren't setting foot in it. It's bad enough that you lot force me to make your weapons and pay me barely half what they're worth, without you sticking your noses where they don't belong."

"Sir, we are the Sheriff's Guard," the second man protested, his nasal whine grating higher in his agitation. "We insist that you step aside and allow us to carry out our search or we'll…"

Rowan heard the shifting of weight as Roderick stepped forward, the scrambling of boots as the guards scuttled back. She imagined Roderick looming over them, hammer held across his chest, face like thunder.

"Or what? Go on, I dare you."

A heavy silence. Rowan could hear the crack and pop of the fire, the slow drip of her sweat onto the surrounding coal.

Finally, one of the guards swallowed noisily. "We… we will be reporting you to our superiors," he said, trying to hide the wobble in his voice and failing miserably. "For… insubordination."

"You do that." Roderick laughed contemptuously. "See where it gets you. Can't make you swords and armour if I'm rotting in a cell now, can I? You won't find another blacksmith willing to accept what your master pays me; I'll tell you that for nothing."

Rowan heard the guard's resentful mutters, the clatter of their footsteps as they hurried away down the street. Soon there was nothing but the whisper of the fire, the distant sounds of the town stirring in its sleep.

"It's alright," Roderick said. "They're gone. You can come out now."

Rowan threw off the covering and scrambled free of the pile in an avalanche of black, coughing and spitting the bitter taste from her mouth. When she straightened up, Roderick was staring at her, his brown eyes round with concern.

"Good god, girl," he sighed, resting his hammer against the wall and running a hand across his close-cropped hair. "What the hell have you got yourself into?"

"You don't want to know," Rowan said, trying to brush the black dust from her clothes.

"You're the one, aren't you?" Roderick said, staring at the hood stitched to her tunic, the mask and scarf hanging around her neck. "You're that 'Green Hood' everyone's been talking about."

Rowan glanced up, meeting his eyes. She'd known Roderick for a long time. He had been a friend of her father. She used to come with him to town so that the two men could talk and laugh and swap deer meat for handfuls of arrowheads. She hadn't seen Roderick since her father died.

"I'm sorry I got you mixed up in this," she said briskly. "It won't happen again."

She glanced out of the open door, into the hungry night beyond. "Do you think they'll come back?"

Roderick gave a low chuckle. "They wouldn't dare. The both of them will be needing a clean pair of britches after tonight."

His laughter died, his face becoming solemn. "Besides, it's like I said. I'm the only one willing to accept the Sheriff's prices. I don't like doing it, but times being what they are, not got a whole lot of other options."

He rubbed at his face with grubby fingers, leaving streaks of soot across his cheeks. "Been burning a lot of midnight oil, I can tell you," he said, gesturing to the piles of swords and half-finished armour. "As have you, from what I hear?"

He eyed Rowan again, his gaze stern. "This thing you're doing, whatever it is," he said. "It's dangerous. What would your poor parents say?"

Rowan felt a surge of anger mixed with guilt. "I wouldn't know, would I? Since they're not here to say it."

Roderick reached out, laid a placating hand on her shoulder. His eyes were suddenly soft again.

"I know you miss them," he said gently. "I do too. Not a day goes by when I don't think of your dad. But this won't bring them back. You'll only get yourself killed."

Rowan shook off his hand and turned away. Her face burned with shame. Her eyes prickled with something else.

"I have to go," she said shortly. "I have to find my friend."

She thought guiltily of Mathew alone in the night-time city. He could have already been arrested or worse.

She glanced back up at Roderick. "Thank you for what you did," she said. "Truly, it means a lot."

She made to go but the big man called her back. "Wait," he said gruffly, turning to rummage on a workbench propped against the wall. "Take this."

He thrust a leather pouch into her hands. It clinked as she took it. Pulling it open, she saw that it was full of arrowheads, gleaming wickedly in the ember glow. She looked up at Roderick, speechless with gratitude. A hand went to her belt, where the last purse of stolen coins hung. Roderick shook his head, stepping away.

"I know what you do with that," he grunted. "Save it for someone who really needs it. Consider it a gift, for old time's sake. I'd much rather you have them than that bastard Sheriff anyway."

He smiled at her, the edges of his eyes crinkling, cracking the soot on his face. Rowan could only stare back, completely at a loss for words. "Hold up," Roderick said as she turned to leave. "They'll have increased the guards on the gates by now. How are you going to get out?"

Rowan suppressed a scowl. She hadn't thought of that.

"I'll think of something."

"No, you won't. At least, not in time."

Roderick stooped, gathering up the fallen swords. He grabbed a couple of brown cloaks from the back of a chair and wrapped them around the bundle.

"Come on. If I can't stop you doing foolish things, I can at least make sure your safe doing them."

❖ ❖ ❖

They found Mathew wandering the streets below the castle, his pale hair glowing like a beacon in the moonlight. Sighing, Roderick bundled them both into the thick cloaks. They had been made for the blacksmith and swallowed them both utterly. Mathew was so small his swept the ground. They were stained liberally with soot, like everything Roderick owned seemed to be.

With some difficulty, Roderick persuaded Rowan to remove her scarf and mask. He insisted that it was necessary for his plan and that the heavy hood would hide her face well enough.

Rowan remained unconvinced. What if the guards demanded to see their faces? What if word had got to them that Gisborne was looking for an auburn-haired girl?

Her stomach skittered and squirmed as they walked through the town, her and Mathew stumbling beneath the weight of the swords Roderick had given them both.

The Blacksmith himself strode ahead, unhampered by his own, much greater burden.

Where's June when you need her? Rowan thought resentfully as they turned into the street leading up to the gates.

She could see that Roderick had been right. A knot of guards now milled around the gates, too many for them to have slipped past.

Her pulse stuttered as one of the guards stepped forwards, hand raised. "What are you doing out so late?" he said.

"Delivery for Locksley Manor," Roderick replied.

Behind his nose guard, the guard frowned. "Odd time to be making a delivery."

Roderick shrugged. "All I know is that I got a message from Sir Guy of Gisborne saying to bring these down soon as possible. You want to go and argue with him about it, feel free. I can wait here all night."

The guard's face blanched at Gisborne's name. He glanced past Roderick at Mathew and Rowan. She tried not to freeze like a cornered forest creature under his gaze.

"Who are they?"

"Just my apprentices," Roderick said with another shrug.

Rowan could feel her scalp itching beneath the heavy hood, sweat tickling the nape of her neck. She took a deep breath and nearly choked on the fabrics stink of smoke and iron.

Beside her, Mathew had set the point of his swords down on the street and was leaning them casually. Rowan did her best to mimic his posture, trying to look bored rather than tense, keeping her eyes downcast so the hood hid her face.

The guard seemed to be making up his mind. Deciding that angering Gisborne was by far the worst possible outcome, he stepped aside and ushered them forward.

"Much obliged," Roderick said with a grin. "Come on, lads."

He strode through the gates, Rowan and Mathew hurrying along behind them. Rowan fought the urge to look back, to check the guards weren't following them. She felt the place between her shoulder blades itch as they carried on down the moonlit road. Only when they were out of sight and arrowshot of the castle did Roderick come to a halt and set down his load.

"Should be ok now."

Rowan and Mathew dropped their bundles with a clatter. Rowan threw off the heavy cloak, breathing in the cool night air. Her chest swelled with relief.

"Thank you," she said, beaming up at Roderick.

The blacksmith's head was lowered as he gathered their swords into his own bundle.

"Least I can do," he muttered. "If you're going to go around trying to get yourself killed…"

But she could hear the smile behind his grumpy tone.

Roderick straightened up, hefting the now much bigger bundle of swords over his shoulders.

Mathew was looking up at him, frowning. "How are you going to get back in?"

"Head around to the south gate and try the same ploy. Say I've got a delivery for the Sheriff and if they want to go wake him up to check then they're welcome."

He grinned, a white slash in the dark. "I was a young scoundrel myself once, you know. I know all the tricks."

Despite everything, Rowan found herself laughing.

"Thanks again," she said, as they prepared to part ways. "For everything."

She touched a hand to the pouch of arrow heads at her belt, her fingers already itching to start on the fine, straight arrows they would make.

Roderick's smile became rueful. "Yeah, well, just try and stay out of trouble, eh?"

Rowan flashed a knife-sharp grin over her shoulder as she and Mathew turned to go. "No promises there."

Roderick's booming laughter followed them as they vanished into the dark.

CHAPTER EIGHT

The outlaws were enjoying a rare moment of peace. Alan was out on watch and the others were in camp, sitting around the fire. Rowan was fletching arrows. June was whittling an offcut of wood. Mathew was working on his latest scheme, using different shaped leaves to stand in place of the Sheriff's men and outlaws.

Suddenly, Alan burst into camp, breathing hard, face flushed and sweating. "Noblewoman," he panted. "On the North Road, travelling alone. If we're quick, we'll reach the first ambush point before she does."

That was all they needed. Without further prompting, they grabbed their weapons and took off through the trees.

Rowan pulled her hood up as she ran, fixing her scarf and mask in place. Her nerves thrummed; her blood sang.

They reached the road and crouched down among the trees at its edge. They waited, watching the trail in silence.

They weren't waiting long. First, there came the clopping of hooves. Then they saw it: a chestnut stallion walking unhurriedly down the road, his coat gleaming in the afternoon sun. On his back sat a young woman.

She was too far off to make out her face, but Rowan could see her long dark hair falling almost to her waist. Her blue gown was simply cut, but Rowan could still tell she was a noble. You always could. It was in the way they held themselves. This girl sat tall and straight, with her head high. It was the posture of someone who had never lived beneath another's heel.

Rowan made a series of hand gestures to the others, telling the boys to go one way, the girls the other. They obeyed at once, moving through the dense undergrowth without as much as a breath to mark their passing. Alan led Mathew with a hand on his arm, as Mathew sometimes struggled to make things out in the forest's patchy light.

She noticed a nearby tree with branches overhanging the road. She smiled to herself. A dramatic entrance always helped to boost the fear factor, and surprise was their best weapon.

She slipped up the tree until she was perched directly above the road. She waited until the noblewoman was right below her. She let out a low, whistling call, like the cry of a bird. As one, Willow and June stepped out in front of the horse. Willow held her bow aloft, arrow nocked and drawn. June hefted her axe menacingly.

The horse whinnied and shied away at their sudden appearance. The noblewoman tried to turn him back the way they had come, only to find Alan and Mathew blocking the road behind her. Alan scowled over his scarf. Mathew's face was eerily blank beneath his hood.

"What is this?" A high note of panic carried through the noblewoman's demanding voice. "Who are you?"

"I'm afraid, my lady, that if you wish to pass through, you must pay a toll," Rowan called out.

The noblewoman's head jerked about, searching for the source of the voice. Rowan jumped down, landing right beside the horse. Its rider started in shock.

"If you prefer, you can think of it as more of a donation," Rowan said.

The noblewoman turned to look at her, and Rowan saw her face for the first time. The shock of it was like a slap. She knew the round curve of that chin, those dark eyes, the raven-curls falling past her shoulders. *Marion!*

"A donation to whom, might I ask?" the girl asked icily. Her face was ferocious, covering her fear with rage.

Rowan tried to shake off her surprise, to slip back into the routine she had practised so many times.

"For the people of Nottingham," she replied, trying to make her voice sound deeper, gruffer, in case Marion recognised it. She could feel the others staring at her in bewilderment. They had never heard her do that before. Her face burned behind the mask

"I'm sure you can spare a little to help them out, my lady," she went on. "And as you can see," she spread her arms to encompass the other outlaws. "You don't have much choice."

Marion glared at her with a hawk-like intensity that Rowan remembered all too well. Then her face relented.

"Very well," she said crisply. She held out a purse. "Here."

Rowan stepped forwards to take it. She didn't want to rob Marion, but if she didn't, the others would want to know why. She reached out her hand for the money.

Rowan would never be able to say how it happened. In less than a second, Marion was off the horse with her arm wrapped around Rowan's neck and a knife jabbed beneath her chin.

"Drop your weapons!" Marion shouted. "Or I'll kill him!"

The others were staring from Marion to Rowan in shocked confusion. Rowan held up a hand to still them. The Marion she knew would never kill anyone, and she was sure this was all just a bluff. Almost sure anyway.

"You don't want to do this, my lady," she said. as calmly as she could.

"I rather think I do," Marion hissed.

"No," Rowan replied, in her own voice again, "Marion, you really don't."

Maybe it was the use of her name, or something familiar in Rowan's voice. Either way, Marion was surprised enough for her grip to slacken slightly. The knife dropped just enough for Rowan to believe that her next hiccup wouldn't be the end of her.

Rowan didn't let the opportunity slip. Grabbing Marion's wrist, she yanked the knife away from her neck. She swept a leg back, taking out Marion's ankles and sending her crashing to the forest floor. Unfortunately, Marion still had a good grip on Rowan's throat and she dragged the other girl choking down with her.

Rowan writhed and shoved, trying to pull away from Marion without hurting her. Marion had no such qualms. She smashed an elbow into the other girl's face, and Rowan felt her nose explode. Jagged light shot behind her eyes. Her scarf soaked through with blood.

"Should we do something?" Alan muttered out of the corner of his mouth.

"I don't know," Mathew said, slightly bemused. "Normally she's won by now."

Marion slashed out with the knife. Rowan gripped her by the wrist and crushed it to the ground until it was forced open and the knife sent skittering away. Marion clawed at Rowan's face, tearing away the mask and scarf, scratching for her eyes. Rowan leaned away from the scrabbling fingers, trying to push Marion back while her feet scrambled to get up.

Marion battered Rowan's hands aside and dived for her again, pinning Rowan to the ground with her knees, wrapping both hands around the other girl's throat, slamming her head against the packed earth of the road. She saw Rowan's face and froze, confusion washing away her fury.

"Rowan?" she gasped.

June seemed to decide that enough was enough. She hauled Marion off Rowan and held her pinned with one arm across the chest. Marion thrashed and fought like a trapped cat, but she was no match for the other girl's strength.

"It's alright, June," Rowan said groggily, stumbling to her feet, blood still spurting from her nose. "You can let her go."

June did so reluctantly, shooting the noble girl a threatening glare.

Marion was staring at Rowan, shock and anger battling for mastery of her face.

Rowan tried out a smile that felt as loose as a broken tooth. She stooped to retrieve Marion's dropped knife and her own discarded scarf and mask. She held out the knife to Marion hilt first.

"Nice to see you too," she said.

Marion took the knife and thrust it back into her belt. She stormed forward and punched Rowan on the arm.

"That's for robbing me!"

"Believe me, I won't be trying it again." Rowan held her scarf up to her bleeding nose, wincing as it throbbed. "Bloody hell, Marion, who taught you to fight?"

"You did."

"Oh yeah…"

Rowan touched a spot on her neck, where Marion's blade had nicked her skin. "Since when do you carry a knife?"

"I was told there are dangerous individuals in the forest these days," Marion said, glaring at Rowan in pure venom. "But I expect you know all about that."

Rowan turned to the others, who were watching the exchange between her and the noble girl in open bewilderment. "Could you give us a moment, please?"

There was something in her voice that told them not to argue. They turned away at once, striding off into the trees, leaving Rowan and Marion alone on the road.

Rowan turned back to Marion and nearly reeled back. She had forgotten how much Marion's glares could burn.

"What is going on? Who are those people? Are you an *outlaw* now?"

The way she said the word 'outlaw' made Rowan's chest clench, as if the term were some awful affliction.

"That's right," she said as casually as she could. "We all are."

"Why? What did you do?"

Rowan didn't want to tell the whole story right now. "Doesn't matter," she said shortly. "When you next see Guy of Gisborne, you'll know."

For a minute, concern flickered across Marion's face. Then her features twisted viciously. "But why didn't you just tell me it was you?" she raged. "Why did you hide your face *and try to rob me?*"

Rowan felt a sudden longing to lay a hand on Marion's arm, to soothe her as she might once have done. But she was too afraid that such a gesture might be unwelcome, that Marion might even find it repulsive. She hitched her usual sardonic smile in place.

"I didn't know you wouldn't betray me. Gisborne wants me dead, and you're a noble, just like him."

Marion looked genuinely hurt. "I would never do that," she said. "Surely you know this."

Her sorrow tugged at Rowan's soul, but she tightened her heart and folded her arms.

"I knew a girl four years ago," she said. "I don't know if you're the same person now."

"I know you're not," Marion shot back, her hurt returning to rage in an instant. "The girl I knew wouldn't have wasted her talents robbing helpless travellers."

"Is it stealing if you're just returning it to who it belongs to?" Rowan could feel her insides simmering, her rage rising to meet Marion's. "Taking from people who can ill-afford it, to pay for a war far away, that's what I call stealing."

"What do you mean?"

"We give it away," Rowan said bluntly. "Every coin we take goes back to the people it was stolen from in the first place. We keep nothing for ourselves."

"And I'm sure you expect nothing in return," Marion said scathingly. "Or do you want to be worshipped like a hero? You're just a common thief."

Rowan turned away, pacing up and down to work out her frustration. She wanted to shake Marion by the shoulders. She wanted to hold her in her arms and never let go. She wanted to run off into the forest and never have to look at her again. She wanted to keep looking at her forever, at her fiery eyes, her soft curls, the gentle curves of her body.

"I've always been a thief," she said instead, firing the words off like arrows. "I had to be, to survive. You never knew what that was like. You don't know what it is to feel so wretched, so helpless, that you must do something, *anything*, to make it stop."

"Then let me help."

The change in Marion's tone was so abrupt it pulled her up short. Rowan turned to stare at her. Marion's face was drawn and pale. Rowan felt a flash of guilt. She hadn't wanted to hurt her, not really.

"I'm heading to Nottingham now," Marion said. "My father wants us to try and gain the Sheriff's favour." She wrinkled her nose in disgust. "I could be your eyes inside the castle, report back what I see and hear. That would be useful, wouldn't it?"

Rowan couldn't deny that it would. Even so, the thought of Marion in danger made her stomach shrivel up.

"Marion, it's too risky. I could never ask you to do that."

"You're not asking, I'm telling you."

"This isn't your fight, you can't…"

"Don't," Marion cut in, her eyes blazing. "Do not tell me I can't do it. Every day, people tell me what I can and cannot do. Do not become one of them, Rowan Fletcher."

She was so fierce and so adamant that Rowan

found herself smiling. *My Marion, the firebrand.* She pushed the thought away. Marion was not *hers*, not in that way.

"OK," she relented. "If you're going to insist on going through with this, then fine, we'll try it. But I can't tell you where our camp is, for your safety as much as ours."

Marion nodded as if she'd expected this. "I'll meet you at the crossroads on the town end of the North Road, the day after tomorrow."

Rowan admired Marion's stubborn jaw, her fierce eyes and felt something twinge inside her. Something like pride, but that wasn't a big enough word.

"Very well," she said, hitching her cocky grin back in place and holding her hand out for Marion to shake. "It's a deal."

CHAPTER NINE

Rowan had thought that the others would head back to camp and she was right. She trudged in, her nose still throbbing, her insides a spikey tangle. The other outlaws stood by the fire, talking in a huddle. They looked up as she approached. Their faces were not friendly. Her spirits sunk further.

"Who was that?" Willow asked.

"Her name is Marion Edwinstowe," Rowan said. "She's a noblewoman."

It wasn't the answer they were after and she knew it.

"You knew her," June rumbled. Her face was dark, her arms crossed. Her words were an accusation.

"Yes," Rowan said, handling each word cautiously. "Her father used to be Lord of Locksley."

"See, that's the thing," June said. "Little Mathew tells us that you only moved into Locksley village four years ago."

Rowan glared at Mathew. His face clouded with shame, and he stared down at his feet. Rowan knew she had no reason to be angry with him. He hadn't said anything that wasn't true, and she'd never told him to keep it to himself. Still, the resentment growled inside her.

"Where were you before then?" asked Alan.

Rowan felt backed into a corner. "That's my business," she said tartly.

"Are you a noble too?" June said, coming right to the point as always.

Rowan gaped at her in astonishment. "What? Of course not! I'm common-born, just like the rest of you."

"Strange, because I don't know any other common-borns who know nobles on a first name basis," June shot back. "How do we know you and your family weren't just disgraced nobles in hiding and that's how you know that girl?"

June's face was thunderous and there was something dangerous gleaming in her eyes. Betrayal. She had grown close to Rowan. Opened up to her. And now she felt as if Rowan had been lying to her.

Rowan sighed. "Look," she said as patiently as she could. "You let me in your gang so I could teach you how to fight and hunt and to help you get back at the Sheriff and his lords. I've done all those things. Doesn't that entitle me to a little privacy?"

Alan and Willow looked as if they were willing to concede the point. June stood scowling, immovable as a mountain.

"Just doesn't seem right," she said. "You know everything about our lives, yet you're keeping this massive part of your own a secret. Why?"

"Because it's none of your concern!" Rowan burst out, her eyes flashing white-hot. "It's my life and I'll keep it to myself if I want to. If you're not happy with that, you can find yourself another archer."

Her words rang through the silent forest. The trees reeled back in shock. For a moment, no one spoke. Even the fire held its breath.

Willow and Alan were glancing at each other, half-afraid. Mathew looked close to tears. June continued to scowl but beneath it, Rowan could sense a sadness. Rowan was June's friend, and Rowan was keeping things from her. Rowan could see how this hurt her more than swords or arrows ever could.

Suddenly, Rowan couldn't face any of them. Muttering something about checking the snares, she turned away and headed back into the forest.

She walked until she reached the spreading elm tree they had used for archery practice. She came here often, to think, to be alone. She clambered up into the tree's fork, resting her back against a branch and breathing in the honeyed smell of sun-warm wood.

She gave a sigh that felt older than every tree in the forest. She was tired and aching from the fight and her nose still pounded. Her stomach felt scraped raw by the thrashing squirm of emotions she was fighting down. She closed her eyes and let them wash over her.

She saw Marion's face, fierce and angry, shocked and afraid, soft and laughing. She remembered her delighted squeals as they raced through the grounds of the manor house as children. She remembered her bright interest as they had walked through the woods together, Rowan naming every tree, pointing out every bird, showing Marion where to gather the best blackberries in autumn, how to set a snare. She saw the look in Marion's dark eyes as she stood in the doorway of her father's manor, watching Rowan walk away.

But we didn't leave her, Rowan thought savagely. She

abandoned us. Her father sent us away and she did nothing.

Not long after Rowan and her parents had left the manor, the Sheriff had passed the governing of Locksley village over to his favourite, Guy of Gisborne. Marion and her father were forced off their lands. They travelled to London, to the King's court. Marion was cousins with the King through her dead mother, and even though he was currently away fighting in a foreign war, the Edwinstowes were still welcome guests at court.

Rowan hadn't seen Marion since the morning she left the manor four years ago. She had thought never to see her again. Now the girl was back and Rowan had no idea how to feel about it.

She remembered a hundred sunlit days, sweet as spring blossom. She thought of stolen moments snatched with Marion. She thought of soft words, gentle hands, warm lips…

"Rowan?"

She jerked free of her memories. She looked down and saw Mathew beneath the tree. He was gazing up at her, eyes wide with worry.

Rowan sighed and swung herself down. She was surprised to see how long the shadows had grown, the sun sinking towards the horizon. How long had she been up there?

Mathew was looking at her in concern. "When you left, you sounded like you wanted to be alone," he said. His voice was cautious, as if every word were a branch he was testing to see if it would take his weight. "And I'll go if you want me to. But I just wanted to say that I'm sorry I told the others about you only living in Locksley for four years. I had no idea it would cause such trouble."

Whatever resentment Rowan had left towards him

melted at the plaintiveness in his eyes.

"It's OK," she said, clasping his shoulder. "I never told you not to. It's not even a secret, not really, it's just… complicated."

Mathew nodded earnestly. "I know you're not a noble; I told the others so. It's just…"

He looked away, searching for the right words. "This is all new to everyone, and we're all scared. I hear it in their voices every day. They're scared for themselves and for the loved ones they left behind. So am I. It's just all so hard."

His words felt heavy on Rowan's soul. She'd had no one to leave behind, no family to worry about. She was still scared though, for the others, of doing something wrong and getting them killed. She was scared for herself too, scared of Gisborne and what he would do if he caught her. And now she was scared for Marion. Marion and her dangerous plan to spy for them, which she had to convince the others was a good idea.

"I know," was all she said.

Mathew chanced a shy smile, and she returned it as best she could.

"It's getting late," he said. "Supper was nearly ready when I left if you want some."

He left the statement open, giving Rowan the chance to refuse if she needed more time to herself. But she was hungry, and she knew she would have to face the others eventually. With a nod, she followed him back to camp.

❉ ❉ ❉

Supper that night was a frosty affair. The others

had spit-roasted a rabbit Rowan had caught earlier, and they'd saved enough for her and Mathew. The echo of harsh words seemed to shiver on the air as they settled down to eat.

The fire chattered loudly, as if the silence made it nervous. The moon rose, and the stars blinked open like weary eyes, and still no one spoke.

Rowan decided it was her job to break the silence. Setting the bones of her rabbit aside, she rested her arms on her knees and took a deep breath.

"Marion has offered to spy for us in Nottingham castle," she said. "We've agreed on a location to meet up the day after tomorrow to exchange information."

"We can't trust her," June said. "She's a *noble*." She spat the final word as if it were the worst insult in the world.

Rowan sighed. To June, nobles were the enemy and always would be. She addressed her next words to the other three, hoping that they would be more reasonable. Marion would go whatever they decided. She would still be risking her life, so it might as well mean something.

"I think it's a good idea," she went on. "It could give us some insight into what the Sheriff's planning, of when and where tax collectors are going to pass through, so we can coordinate our attacks better. She wants to help and I think we should let her."

"And you think we can rely on her not betraying us?" Willow asked.

"I know we can," Rowan replied. "I know *her*. She won't sell us out."

As she spoke, her own words floated back to her on the evening breeze. *I knew a girl four years ago...* Marion had spent those four years at court, with the King's toxic younger brother and his corrupt lords. Who knew what she had become now?

No, came a small insistent voice in her head. *She's not like that, not my Marion.* Another voice came, just as insistent but much darker. *She was never yours, not in that way. Who knows whose she is now?*

"So, you know her, but you can't tell us how?" Alan asked.

Rowan gave another sigh. "Not yet, no. It's complex and personal. I will, one day, just not right now."

Alan chewed on this. He looked half-convinced. Willow looked reluctant. June continued to glower at everyone.

"Well, I think it's a great idea," Mathew piped up.

"You think everything Rowan suggests is a great idea," Willow muttered, picking up a stick and digging it into the ground.

"No, I don't, but this is! Having eyes in the castle will be incredibly good for our campaign."

"Since when did we become a campaign?" Willow asked, incredulous, but Rowan could tell the other girl wasn't fighting her anymore.

Willow gave a great sniff and then a sigh. "Alright," she said at last. "If you can swear she's trustworthy, then I say let's give her a shot."

"I swear," Rowan replied. "I'll break my bow if I'm wrong."

As she said the words, she realised she meant them. She felt a little surer.

Alan nodded to show he agreed too. Mathew was beaming, though whether this was because of this new development in his machinations, or because everyone was getting along again, it was unclear.

"Hold up," said June. She was still scowling and Rowan braced herself for another argument. "I can see that I'm going to be outvoted again. I'll agree on one condition."

She turned her scowl on Rowan, who tried not to flinch. "When you go to meet her, I'm going with you," she said. "Whatever you say of this girl, I don't trust her. It would be too easy to set up a trap once she's got you on your own. At least if I come, there'll be someone to watch your back."

Rowan nodded, speechless. That June cared about her that much, after only knowing her for a few months… She thought her chest might burst with gratitude.

The others bedded down for the night. Rowan offered to take the first watch. Her mind was spinning too much to sleep. All she could think, as the fire burned down to embers and the stars spun in their slow dance overhead, was *I'll see Marion again in two days.* It fizzed in her blood and spiked in her stomach. She sat and watched the moon climb the sky.

CHAPTER TEN

By the time Marion reached Nottingham, it was near dark. She brushed off her father's scolding with the insistence that she had merely gotten distracted on her ride through the woods and lost track of time. He had gone ahead in a carriage, but she had insisted on riding through the forest. She had missed the woods while they had been at court and had wanted some time to herself to think. She hadn't bargained on being given so much to think about.

Her head still spinning, she was introduced to the Sheriff of Nottingham and Sir Guy of Gisborne. It had been her father's idea for the pair of them to spend some time at the castle, in the hope of getting into the Sheriff's good graces. He was hoping to find her a husband too, but she tried not to think about that. The very idea made her chest feel like it was wrapped in iron bands.

As soon as Marion saw Sir Guy, she could see what Rowan meant. A long scar marked his handsome face. A patch covered one eye. That coupled with the wandering gaze of his remaining eye, the twist to his smile when he saw her, and it was easy to see why her friend was now an outlaw.

She remembered Gisborne from before she went to London, an ambitious young lord eager to get into the Sheriff's favour. There were all kinds of stories of what dark deeds he had done to get there.

Marion felt the weight of her knife, small but sharp, concealed in a pocket she had sewn into the inside of her dress. It was only the thought of it, the idea of thrusting it through Gisborne's hand whenever it lingered too long on her arm, that stopped her from running from the room and scrubbing her skin clean over and over.

The Sheriff was a complete contrast. He was a mild, unassuming looking man with a mild, unassuming manner. He was not particularly tall, with mousy coloured hair and a neat little beard. He greeted Marion politely, introducing her to the other lords and ladies who orbited him. But still, there was something about him, something behind the fine words and courtly gestures, which put Marion on edge. It was his eyes, she decided. They were as cold and flat as those of a dead thing.

The evening wore on, in a blur of too-rich food and too-loud laughter. Despite the mild summer night, a huge log fire blazed in the hearth. Hundreds of candles lit the hall, only adding to the heat. Thick tapestries hung from the walls, cutting out any hint of a draft from the outside world. The air was so thick that Marion felt as if she were drowning in honey.

She tried to focus on the conversations around her, listening out for anything useful.

"This interminably dry weather," the lord to her left was saying. "My land will be quite useless if we don't get some rain soon."

"Indeed," said his neighbour. "I'm having very low yields this year. It's intolerable."

"I've had to increase my household guard," said another, taking a sip of wine. "You know how the rabble get restless when food is short."

The conversation was disrupted when the finely dressed lady to Marion's right gave a shriek of displeasure. Marion turned to see that she had spilled wine down the bodice of her gown.

"Damn it," she said, dabbing at herself furiously. "This dress took weeks to make. I'll have that serving boy whipped."

The boy in question, hovering a few feet away with a pitcher of wine, blanched and scurried away. He had been nowhere near the noblewoman when the accident occurred and Marion opened her mouth to say as much.

Her father silenced her with a glare. As far as he was concerned, they were here to gain favour, not cause trouble.

Marion sighed, rubbing a hand over her eyes. Sweat was beginning to pool in the base of her spine. She was just about to make her excuses and leave when Rowan was mentioned. At first, she didn't realise the lord to the Sheriff's left was even talking about her friend.

"The 'Green Hood', they're calling him," the lord chortled, clearly deep in his cups. "Apparently, he gives away all he steals."

He laughed uproariously. "Have you ever heard of such a thing? Not much of a bandit, is he? Certainly not a rich one."

Marion stiffened. She fought to keep her face neutral.

"It's not a joke, Thembsford," another lord said, his face grave. "The people look up to him. If he asked them to rise up and stick our heads on spikes, they would. He's dangerous, you mark my words."

"Oh, come now," said Thembsford jovially. "An uprising? Not likely is it. They lack the organisation for one thing."

"Or the intelligence," someone else offered, to the general pleasure of the table.

"The only thing this Green Hood seems capable of doing," Thembsford added, clapping the Sheriff on the back, "is making our friend here look a fool. How much of your coin has he stolen now, eh d'Aubigny?"

An icy quiet settled over the table. A smile appeared on the Sheriff's sallow face, like a slit in paper. His eyes were cold fury.

"Nothing we cannot replace," he replied, in a measured tone that seared like frostbite. "And we have already doubled patrols of the forest. We'll have this Green Hood hanging from the city gates before too long, I assure you."

"I wouldn't count on it," Thembsford chuckled. "It's vast, the forest. You could search it for a hundred years and never find him. They know how to hide, these woodsman types."

Now Gisborne spoke. He was languid where the Sheriff was rigid, lounging in his chair like a lion among men. "He can't hide forever. He enjoys the spotlight too much. That will be his undoing. To give money to the peasants, he has to leave his hidey-hole. That is how we will catch him."

"If it's even one man," another lord piped up, a thin, ratty man with nervous eyes. "How do we know it's not many bandits all adopting the same pseudonym? What if the forest is crawling with them?"

"Fear not, my Lord Chester," the Sheriff said. "I will

personally guarantee the safety of anyone who grants me fealty. We are recruiting new guardsmen all the time and increasing the protection detail for any traveller passing through the forest. Your money will be quite safe, believe me."

A promise but also a threat. Stay loyal or be thrown to the wolves.

Marion had finally heard something of some use, so now she could go. If she remained in this oppressive opulence any longer, she might scream.

She told her father she would see him back at the manor. She slipped out into the cool corridor. She sighed, breathing in the soothing silence. She turned to head back to the stables.

"Lady Marion."

She froze, her heart stuttering. Her escape hadn't been as subtle as she had hoped. She turned, her stomach clenching at the sight of Guy of Gisborne. He stepped into the corridor, closing the door behind him, muffling the noise of the feast inside.

"Leaving so soon?" he asked, eyebrows arching.

Marion forced her face into what she hoped was a demure smile. "I have a slight headache. I thought it would be best to go home and rest."

"I could accompany you if you wish," Sir Guy suggested, leaning against the wall with arms folded, a leering grin sneaking up his face. "A young woman should not be travelling alone after dark. We live in dangerous times, my lady."

I have no doubt, Marion thought, watching the gleam in Gisborne's eye as his gaze crawled over her.

Her hand rested on the concealed knife. Oh, how she wished to pull it free, to sink it into the Lord's remaining eye, to twist and twist until his screams split the stones.

"That is very kind of you," she forced the words out, though they burned her mouth. "But quite unnecessary. I rode here alone and besides, some of my father's servants came with us. One of them will ride back with me."

Gisborne did not back down. "Are you sure? It would be no trouble. If you rather, you could stay here for the night. There are plenty of rooms spare."

"No," Marion said, too quickly. "Thank you, but it is quite alright. I will head back."

If Marion had hoped this would deter Gisborne, she was mistaken. He straightened up from the wall and stepped forwards. He loomed over her, stinking of leather and sweat.

"You know, it is a mystery to me how a lady as well connected and… finely featured as yourself could go so long unwed."

There was a caress to his voice that made Marion's whole being shudder. She stepped back, out of his reach.

"Might I ask, Sir Guy, how you got that scar?" she asked sweetly. "I don't recall you having it the last time we met."

That threw him. Gisborne's hand crept to his face. Something like anger flickered across his features.

"It… was an accident," he replied.

"An accident?"

"Yes," he insisted. "A hunting accident."

A look stole over his face, a terrifying, hungry ferocity. Marion felt her insides go cold. She thought of Rowan, alone in the woods, with only her little band of outlaws to keep her safe. She wished they had planned to meet sooner, so she could warn them.

"It is getting late. I had best be going," she said, eager to get as far away from this man as she could. "Goodnight, Sir Guy."

Without giving him time to stop her, she turned and hurried away, through the castle and out into the summer-scented night.

CHAPTER ELEVEN

"I don't like this."

"You've mentioned."

"It's too exposed. Could easily be an ambush."

"Nothing to stop you just going back to camp."

June scowled. "Not likely."

Rowan sighed. They were crouched on the edge of the forest, still hidden within the treeline. Ahead of them lay the crossroads, their meeting point with Marion. She hadn't arrived yet, and June refused to step into the open until she had seen the noble girl. Rowan didn't have the energy to argue anymore, and she had to admit it wasn't a bad plan.

She shifted nervously, trying to relieve the ache in her cramped limbs. The last day and a half had been the longest of Rowan's life. She had found it impossible to focus on anything. Marion's face filled her mind whenever she tried. The familiar tangle of feelings had been tearing her insides apart.

Now she felt jumpy and tense, as if before a battle. Her body was desperate to move, to run, to *do something.*

Finally, the sound of hooves rang out through

the still air and a lone rider appeared, coming from the direction of town. Rowan's stomach did a backflip as Marion reined her horse in at the crossroads and dropped down from his back. She stood beside him, holding the reins and looking around her, face tight with anticipation.

Rowan made to get up, to run out to her. June stopped her with a strong hand.

"We should wait," she said. "See if anyone else turns up."

"And then what?" Rowan snapped. "We wait until she decides we're not coming and leaves? She might have something important to tell us. There's such a thing as too much caution, you know."

With that, Rowan shook off June's hand and strode out into the open. She heard muffled grumbling as June got to her feet and hurried after her.

Rowan pulled away her mask and scarf as she walked. Marion spun at the sound of her approach, the fear on her face quickly replaced by relief when she recognised her old friend. Rowan felt a flutter of joy at the expression and quickly stamped it down. She didn't want her feelings to be dictated by the whims of this girl.

"You came," Marion breathed. "I was beginning to fear that maybe you wouldn't."

"I make it a policy to keep my promises," said Rowan, letting a sly smile curl the edge of her words, "when I can."

June took her place beside Rowan. She had not bothered to remove the scarf covering the lower half of her face, and she was glowering at Marion, hefting her axe in both hands.

"This is June," Rowan said, resigned, seeing the

anxious glances Marion was throwing at the taller girl. "I don't believe proper introductions were made the other day."

June shot Rowan a murderous glance, but Rowan ignored it. Marion hadn't sold them out, so Rowan didn't see what harm giving her one more name would do.

"Pleased to meet you," Marion said shyly.

June did not respond, just continued to glare in stony-faced revulsion.

"Anyway," said Rowan. "Do you have anything for us?"

She almost said *anything for me* and had to fight back a blush when she realised how that would sound.

Marion nodded. "I didn't get much, but you should know that the Sheriff is planning on doubling the men he has patrolling the forest."

Rowan nodded. It was unwelcome news, but not unexpected.

"He's increasing the number of guards on the convoys travelling the roads too," Marion added. "The lords are getting worried about their money. They're even more worried that you're going to incite some sort of rebellion."

Rowan felt another grin quirk her mouth. "So, we're making an impact?"

"You need to be careful." Marion's tone surprised her. It was low, anxious, her eyes wide and imploring. "I saw Sir Guy. I saw what you… what happened…"

"He deserved it," Rowan snapped, more harshly than she meant to.

"I don't doubt that." There was a bitterness to Marion's voice that made Rowan sure she meant it. "But you need to watch your step. I saw his face when I asked about the scar. If he catches you, I don't know what he'll do."

Rowan remembered hard hands grinding the bones of her wrist together, the weight of his body against hers, his scream as she sliced the arrowhead across his eye. She suppressed a shudder.

Marion was talking once more. "He knows about you giving away what you take. I think he plans to lay a trap for you, or the "Green Hood" as they call you. He's determined to catch you."

"He doesn't know I'm the Green Hood," Rowan replied. "No one does, except you, and I trust you to keep it a secret."

She flashed Marion her most winning smile. But Marion glared back with all her hawk-sharp ferocity.

"That won't matter when he catches you, will it?"

"He won't catch me."

"You don't know that!" Marion's voice was turning shrill. "You don't know him like I do, what he's capable of…"

"I don't care," Rowan said, her volume rising with her temper. "I'm not going to stop what I'm doing. It's the most worthwhile thing I've ever done and I'm not letting him take that from me."

"I know that," Marion cried. "I just don't want to lose you again, not after…"

She broke off, looking scared, as if afraid she'd said the wrong thing. Rowan wondered how she was going to finish that sentence. After what? After so long apart? After everything that had happened? Her heart gave a tiny leap. Was it possible that Marion felt the same as she did? It seemed unlikely, after all this time, but still…

"Ok," she said, her voice softer. She longed to

take Marion's hand but she held back. "I'll be careful. I promise."

Marion nodded, sniffing slightly. She gazed at Rowan with eyes as deep, dark blue as moonless nights and dreamless sleep.

Rowan felt she could drown in eyes like that. She looked away, feeling heat rise to her face. She half-wished she still had her mask and scarf to hide it.

"So, er, how was court?" she asked, groping desperately for a new topic of conversation.

Marion wrinkled her nose. "Full of posturing young lords with no sense and too much pride."

"You should have just demonstrated your skill with a knife." Rowan grinned, rubbing the scab on her neck. "I'm sure that would have seen them off."

Marion smiled, a small and thin smile, but it still made Rowan's blood sing. There was a time when she would have done anything for that smile. But now… now things were different. She had far more important things to worry about than the feelings of a noblewoman.

Beside her, June gave a grunt of impatience. Rowan knew she was right. They had been exposed for too long. It was time to get back under cover.

"Thank you for coming to tell me this," she said to Marion. "I know it can't have been easy."

Marion nodded eagerly. "I can come again. The Sheriff is having another dinner in two days. I can see if I can find out anything else and bring it to you the following morning."

Unwilling as Rowan was for Marion to put herself in more danger, she couldn't deny that the information she had brought so far had been useful. She gave a reluctant nod.

"Same time, same place?"

Marion agreed.

Rowan turned to leave, but then she looked back, something occurring to her.

"If you ever need me," she began, voice faltering and cautious. "I mean... if anything ever goes wrong, if you ever need a place to hide, then come to the woods. Make a call like an owl during the day or like a woodpigeon if it's night. Like I showed you when we were little, remember?"

Marion nodded.

"Just keep making the call, and I'll... I'll find you."

Rowan gazed at Marion, wanting to say more, wanting to say everything, but she couldn't find the words. Marion was looking back at her, dark eyes wide and soft. Under their gaze, Rowan's voice curled up in a scared ball at the back of her throat.

Instead, she muttered, "It was good to see you again, Marion," before turning and following June back into the trees.

"So, you two were *friends*?" June said after a few moments walking in silence. Rowan didn't need to look at her friend's face to feel the scepticism. "Tell me, how does a noblewoman make friends with a peasant girl anyway?"

Rowan sighed. It was clear that June wasn't going to let this drop until she had a satisfactory answer. Since she had risked a lot by coming today, Rowan decided that she deserved a bit of honesty.

"We grew up together," she said, fixing her mask and scarf back into place as they walked. "Back when her father was Lord of Locksley. When my dad came back from the war, he and my mum took serving jobs at the manor. Dad was the gamekeeper, Mum worked in the kitchens. I helped out however I could, in the stables mostly."

"Marion and I were the same age, the only children in the whole place. Whenever I was done with my work and she could escape from her lessons, we ran wild in the house's grounds. I showed her how to track, how to shoot, how to fight, just like my father taught me. She taught me how to read and write. I'd have never learned otherwise."

Rowan paused, lost in endless summer days bright with sunlight and laughter. And then a shadow crossed her mind.

"Then d'Aubigny became Sheriff and started lining his pockets with the higher taxes. Marion's father decided he couldn't afford to keep on so many servants. My family was sent away, back to Locksley village."

She gulped, remembering that morning four years ago. She remembered walking away from the manor, looking back and seeing Marion on the doorstep. She remembered the wrenching pain of it, as if a part of her was being torn away.

"Not long after that, the Sheriff gave the manor and control of the village over to Sir Guy of Gisborne, and Marion and her father left for the King's court in London. I didn't think I'd ever see her again."

She licked her dry lips. Her next words were the most painful, but she found that now she had started she couldn't stop.

"My family was left with nothing, scraping to survive. My dad started hunting in the forest, just to put food on the table. And that worked until… until last summer, when he was caught and hanged for poaching."

Rowan felt the heat of that morning beating like a lash on her back. She saw the jerking dance of her father's legs, heard his terrible, gurgling gasps as the noose tightened. She heard her mother sobbing beside her. She saw Gisborne, the one who had proclaimed her father's guilt, standing beside the scaffold. She felt his eyes find her, saw the cruel glint of his smile.

She shook her head, jerking herself back to the present. June was looking at her, her eyes deep with sorrow.

"Mum died in the winter," Rowan choked out, forcing back the sobs clawing up her throat. "Without Dad's hunting, we didn't have enough to eat and she got sick and…"

She broke off, remembering a cold so fierce it could eat the flesh off your bones. She remembered a hunger so deep it was like a living thing tearing you apart from the inside. She saw her mother lying in bed, thin and pale as the sheets. She felt her mother's cold hand in hers, felt the last flutterings of a pulse fade away.

It was after this that Rowan had stopped caring too much about what happened to her. She had already lost everything. Her life didn't feel like such a significant thing on top of that. She had begun to hunt the forest with reckless abandon, dividing the meat up among the other villagers. It had felt like a defiance, to Gisborne and the Sheriff and their stupid, pointless laws. It had felt like a duty, to make sure no one else suffered the same fate her parents had.

She looked into June's face; her broad features soft with concern. Rowan forced a smile, thin and shuddery as melting ice.

"So now you know my big secret," she said. "You can tell the others if you want." She couldn't face recounting the story again, but she knew it would probably be good for them to hear it as well.

"But I know Marion," she added. "She's not like other nobles. We can trust her, I promise."

June sniffed and looked away. "We'll see."

Rowan found herself laughing. "What else does she have to do to prove herself to you? Bring us the Sheriff's head on a platter?"

"That would be helpful."

"Well, she might if she's forced to marry one of his lords. She was never one for doing what she was told."

June looked at her friend with raised eyebrows. "So, you do have a lot on common."

Rowan laughed, punching June playfully on the shoulder as together they stepped off the road and headed back to camp.

CHAPTER TWELVE

It was Marion who told them about the archery contest, but it took Mathew to see the opportunity it held.

"The prize is three hundred pounds" he said. "That's enough to feed a village for a year at least!"

Rowan, who was sat on a tree stump oiling her bow, did not look up.

"I mean, it's clearly a trap," she said. "Not even a subtle one. The sheriff has no intention of handing over that money. He's just going to arrest whichever poor sap wins thinking it's me."

She held up her bow, pulling back the string to check its suppleness.

"Well, obviously," Mathew said. "I'm not suggesting for a moment that you enter. But still, all that money in one place, it's too great an opportunity to miss."

Rowan looked up with raised eyebrows. Mathew had that devious glint in his eye that she had come to associate with imminent danger.

"What are you suggesting?"

* * *

"Are you completely unhinged?" Marion raged. "This is so obviously a ploy to catch you. Are you really so obtuse not to see that or just too arrogant?"

"Neither," Rowan said calmly. "The idea isn't that I enter. We plan to play the Sheriff at his own game."

It had been two weeks since Marion had returned. They had continued to meet up regularly, always at a different location, so that she could pass on what she had learned.

Today, they were by a ruined chapel on the edge of the forest. They were alone, June finally deciding that Marion didn't pose a significant enough danger that she needed to be there all the time, for which Rowan was grateful.

"The idea is to use this as an opportunity," Rowan went on. "There's never that much money in one place, not out in the open. I'll use the archery contest to create a diversion, drawing the guards away, then the others will nab the prize-pot while no-one's watching. We get the money, the Sheriff looks a fool, everyone's happy."

"You shouldn't bait him so," Marion said. "He's not a stray dog you can tease. He's dangerous."

"You think I don't know that?" Rowan said sharply. Her father's face was flashing across her mind, his last gurgling breaths echoing in her ears.

Marion's face clouded with shame and she looked down at the ground. Rowan felt a pang of guilt for speaking so harshly. Marion had been close with Rowan's parents and she had only found out about their deaths a few days ago.

"I just mean, you shouldn't underestimate him," she said. "Nor his desperation to be rid of you. The reward on your head is up to one hundred now…"

"A hundred and fifty," Rowan corrected, the ghost of a grin quirking her lips.

Marion shot her a glare. "I'm sorry, are you *enjoying* being the most wanted person in Nottingham?"

Rowan shrugged, side-ways smile sliding up her face. "Well, I'm *not* not enjoying it."

Marion gave a huff of frustration. "I should turn you in myself, use the money to do some real good."

"Probably, but we both know you won't," Rowan said, still grinning. "You'd miss me too much."

Marion's eyes met hers and Rowan felt her insides give a twinge, the look tugging on an old wound. She swallowed, shaking herself mentally.

"So, will you be attending the contest?" she asked with an air of casualness.

"Yes. Gisborne's asked me along as his *personal guest*." Marion wrinkled her nose in disgust.

Rowan's insides went volcanic. The idea of a man like Gisborne anywhere *near* Marion was repugnant.

"Can't you just turn him down?" she said, the words coming out more harshly than she had meant them to.

"I wanted to," Marion sighed. "But my father insisted. He had to bow and scrape enough to the Sheriff just for him to grant us Wolfstone, and he fears losing even that if we're not suitably *compliant*." She spat the last word as if it tasted bitter.

Wolfstone Manor was an old hunting lodge, tucked away in the woods not far from Nottingham. It had none of the grandeur of Locksley Hall and a fraction of the grounds, but it was the only home Marion and her father had been granted upon their return. Marion was unbothered by the arrangement, but it was clear that her father rankled at the loss of status.

"Gods, imagine you not being compliant," Rowan grinned. "Next you'll be telling me you're consorting with outlaws."

For a moment, Marion actually smiled back and Rowan felt her heart give a little skip. Then the other girl schooled her face back into a scowl.

"Speaking of which, I don't suppose you're planning on telling me exactly what it is you plan to *do* at the contest?" she said. "So that I'm forewarned."

Rowan let her smile spread. "Now where would be the fun in that?" she said. "Don't worry, you won't miss it. It promises to be quite… *spectacular*."

With a final glint of grin, she vanished into the trees.

* * *

Rowan crouched lower on the rooftop, using the slope of the thatch to hide her from view. Below, there came the twang of a bowstring, the thud of an arrow in wood and the polite applause of the watching crowd.

The archery contest was taking place in the square before the castle gates, which was normally used for executions. Indeed, the scaffold on its platform had been repurposed as a stage, the target at the far end.

The contest was open to everyone, peasant or noble, in the sheriff's futile attempt to flush out the Green Hood. So far, the majority of the contestants had been noblemen, but a few peasant hunters and gamekeepers had shown up too and fared well. But so far, no-one had shot with the flair the Green Hood was known for.

Rowan chanced another peek over the roof's peak. At the far side of the square, she could make out the Sheriff. He sat watching the proceedings from a raised dais. The prize pot, a small, sturdy chest packed with gold and silver, sat at his boots. Two armed guards stood before it. It had been shown off at the beginning of the contest, an attempt for d'Aubigny to show he was in earnest.

The Sheriff's face was inscrutable, but at his side, Gisborne was growing visibly agitated, shifting in his seat, his glower deepening with every mediocre shot. Beside him, Marion sat with a rigid back, her face smoothly blank. Anyone who didn't know her might have seen any other noble woman's haughty disdain for the proceedings, but Rowan knew better. Marion would be scouring the crowd for Rowan and the others, straining for any sign of what their plan might be.

Rowan allowed herself a secret smile. Marion would be disappointed. The other outlaws had slipped into the crowd and were slowly getting themselves into position. Mathew had a cloth cap pulled over his distinctive hair. June wore the rough clothes of a labourer; her skin streaked with soot so she resembled a charcoal burner. Willow's dark hair was lightened by ash, her back bent and crooked as an old woman, swamped by a shapeless grey cloak. There was little chance of even someone they knew recognising them, which was the intention.

Rowen herself had been smuggled through the gates in a beggars disguise, using one of Roderick's enormous brown cloaks again to hide her face and clothes. Soon as they were out of sight of the guards, the cloak had come off, her mask and scarf back on and she had slipped through the shadows of the town's backstreets until she had come to the square and found this perch.

The last contestant mounted the platform and Rowan's senses sharpened. Slowly, silently, she drew her bow and nocked an arrow. Her blood was spiking, her stomach fizzing.

She watched the man draw back his blow. She breathed in deep, let it out slow, calming her nerves, slowing her pulse.

He let fly. The arrow thudded into the target, almost hitting the centre but not quite. There was a disappointed groan from the crowd, followed by muted applause. Rowan made out the faintest frown flicker across the Sheriff's face as he got to his feet, ready to proclaim the winner.

In one movement, Rowan shot upright, drew back her bow and loosed the arrow. It flew straight and true, zipping across the square and thudding into the centre of the target.

A gasp rippled through the crowd. Everyone began looking around the square, searching for where the arrow had come from.

Gisborne was on his feet, a predator coiled to spring. Marion's face had gone two shades paler.

Rowan felt the smallest speck of guilt, but she swallowed it down. Ears ringing, she filled her lungs and shouted in her deepest, loudest voice.

"Does this mean I win, Sheriff?"

Every head snapped around to her, faces wide with shock to see the hooded and masked figure perched like some weird bird on the rooftop.

Gisborne's face was a picture of fury. The Sheriff's eyes were cold as he called to his guards.

"Seize him!"

The dozen or so guardsmen posted around the square, including, Rowan noted, the two guarding the chest, moved forward as one. Gisborne sprung from the dais. Rowan took off running, leaping the gap to the next roof and flying away down the street.

Her blood sang as she leapt from rooftop to rooftop. Below, the clank and stomp of perusing guards were being left far behind. Her heart soared. They would never catch her now!

She leapt the next gap. The second her boots hit the thatch; it gave way beneath her. She crashed down in a shower of mouldy straw and splintered wood. She hit the boards beneath, the impact punching all the air from her.

She lay on her back, gasping, staring up at the hole in the ceiling above her. The rafters must have rotted through, leaving nothing to support the thatch above. She was lying in someone's hayloft.

She sat up stiffly, rolling her shoulders with a groan. Everything ached, but nothing seemed broken. There was a crash below her as the front door flew open. She stared down into Gisborne's burning blue eye.

Panic knifed through the paralysis of shock. She sprung up, sprinting for the window at the far end of the hayloft, the shutters thrown open to let in the summer breeze. But Gisborne had already lunged for the ladder leading to the hayloft. He leaped up, grabbed her ankle. She went sprawling, the breath knocked from her lungs a second time as her chest hit the boards.

She kicked out, trying to free herself, but Gisborne

was half-way up the ladder by now. He leaned forward, crushing her legs with his weight. He grabbed her belt, used it to drag himself up the rest of the way.

Rowan writhed and thrashed beneath him. Panic clawed her throat. This was too much like the last time. The crushing weight of him, his hot leather stink choking her, his bruising hands reaching for her hood.

No, no, this couldn't be like last time, it couldn't be! With a super-human effort, she twisted onto her back, thrusting her hood out of his grip. But he was fully on her now, his knees pinning her legs, hand groping for her face.

His fingers hooked in her scarf and she lashed out desperately, catching his jaw with her elbow. She heard him grunt at the impact, felt the scarf tear as she twisted her head to one side. She kept going, fists and elbows landing in a mad flurry, not giving him time to think. He growled in anger. He struck out wildly, his fist clipping her jaw so hard she saw stars. By the time she had blinked them away, he had ripped his dagger free and had it raised above her heart.

The blade came down. Rowan fastened both her hands around his wrist, forcing it back. The dagger quivered between them, inches from Rowan's chest. Gisborne reached his spare hand for her mask. His single eye gleamed in triumph. He was going to be the one to unmask the Green Hood once and for all.

Rowan tried to push his reaching hand away, but she couldn't hold the dagger at bay one handed. The point dipped lower. Rowan gave a breathless cry as it scraped down her collarbone, tearing her tunic and spilling red.

Her breath came loud and sharp. Her heart bruised her ribs. Gisborne's fingers brushed her mask. She desperately tried to twist her head away. Hot blood slithered against her skin. In one last, frantic effort, she kicked a leg free and brought the knee up as hard as she could into Gisborne's groin.

He gave a startled yelp, his body folding inwards. She kicked him again and he rolled off her, curling over the affected region like a snail in its shell.

Rowan scrambled to her feet, sweating and breathless. She glanced back at Gisborne, helpless and groaning on the floor. Her own words flashed through her, vivid as lightning. *If he comes near me again, I'll kill him.*

No time to see if she'd meant them. The other guards had caught up, were filling the house like a clanking flood, pointing up at Rowan and dashing for the ladder. Rowan sprinted for the open window. Jumping up onto the sill, she saw that she had reached the very edge of Nottingham, where the town met the forest. She could see the branches of the trees protruding over the town walls, like welcome arms, reaching out to catch her.

Quick as thought, she scrambled up onto the roof, ran to the edge and leapt. She hit the nearest tree, grabbing for branches and wrapping her legs around the trunk, heedless of scratches or grazes. She scrambled down the tree and disappeared into the forest. By the time the first guard reached the window, she was long gone.

❋ ❋ ❋

Rowan leaned against a tree, gasping for breath, one hand pressed to the cut at her collarbone.

She had run until she could go no further. Now she was deep in the forest, far away from the town. The trees were spaced widely here, sunlight streaming down through the canopy. From nearby came the chuckle of a stream.

She looked around, trying to judge where she was. The plan had been that once Mathew and the others had pilfered the prize money; they were going to meet up back at camp. However, Rowan appeared to now be on the complete opposite side of the forest to where that was.

She sighed, pushing herself off the tree. She winced as her wound gave a twinge. She had a long walk ahead of her, and while the cut was shallow, it still pounded like a second heartbeat.

Behind her, the sound of a throat clearing. Rowan jumped, spun around, one hand reaching for her bow, hissing as the sudden movement tugged on her wound. Marion stood before her, arms folded, face sharp with ferocity. Rowan hadn't even heard her approach.

She let out a breath, leaning back against the tree.

"Well, that went swimmingly," Marion said, voice icy.

"All according to plan," Rowan said, straightening up and flashing her sharp-edged grin.

"Was standing around in the open waiting to get captured part of the plan?" Marion snapped. "Was that?"

She gestured angrily to the red stain seeping through Rowan's tunic. Rowan raised a hand to cover to wound.

"It's nothing," she insisted. "Just a scratch. Willow will fix it up, no problem."

"Let me see." Marion strode over, pulling Rowan's hand aside to examine the cut. Rowan remained still as Marion pulled back the torn layers of bloody cloth to expose the wound beneath.

"You can't go gallivanting across the forest with it open like this," she tutted. "You'll only make it worse. Come on."

Taking Rowan by the arm, she led her down to the stream, sitting her down on a mossy rock at the water's edge. She told Rowan to remove her tunic while she went to get supplies. Rowan did so, wincing. Her undershirt clung to her skin, sticky with sweat and drying blood.

Marion returned, carrying a bundle of cobwebs in a dock leaf in one hand. Setting the bundle down, she gently untied the laces of Rowan's shirt, pulling the collar down to expose the wound. Rowan did her best not to flinch when the fabric was pulled away from where it had stuck to the cut, not to shudder at the softness of Marion's hands.

"This brings back memories," she muttered, before she could stop herself.

Marion's face flushed scarlet. "Scarf," she said, as if Rowan hadn't spoken, holding out her hand imperiously.

Rowan pulled the strip of green from her neck. It was torn from the fight with Gisborne, both ends hanging ragged and unravelling, but it would still serve its purpose.

She handed it over. Marion stooped, soaking the scarf in the stream before bringing it back up to the wound. Rowan hissed at the first touch of the icy water.

"Did you ever think of me?" she asked, more to keep her mind off the pain than anything else. "While you were away?"

Marion's face flushed darker. She kept wiping away the blood, not looking up from her work.

"Did you think of me?" she shot back.

"Of course I did," Rowan said, the softness of her voice surprising even her. "Marion, what we had... what we were..."

Marion wrung out the scarf in a shower of pinkish droplets. "We were young," she said tartly. "And foolish."

"Without a doubt," Rowan agreed. "But that didn't make it any less real. You can't tell me it meant nothing to you. Why else did you evade the charms of all those young lords at court?"

"You wouldn't be asking that if you'd actually met any of them," Marion muttered, picking up the bundle of cobwebs and pulling apart the sticky strands.

"Aren't we done with this?" Rowan's voice was half a plea. "Ever since you came back, we've been angry with each other for things neither of us could help. I was cross with you for leaving, even though it wasn't your choice. And you've been angry with me for refusing to be another of the Sheriff's boot-scrapers..."

She bit back a cry as Marion began sticking the cobweb strands down more zealously then was strictly necessary.

"For being reckless," Marion fumed, glaring at the wound as she continued to stick it shut. "For taking unnecessary risks for the sake of fame and glory."

Rowan raised an eyebrow. "If you hate what I do so much, why do you help me?"

"I don't hate it!" Marion glared up at her. "I never denied that what you did was important, essential even. But why does it have to be you? Why do you have to be the one risking life and limb? Why not… someone else?"

There was a hitch in her voice as she finished, a brightness in her eyes.

Rowan looked at her steadily, her voice calm and level. "Because there is no-one else."

Marion stared back at her, then turned away, rubbing at her eyes furiously.

"Anyway," Rowan added with a sideways smile as Marion turned back to her work. "Why do you care what happens to me, if you've not given me a second thought in four years?"

Marion glowered, slapping the last of the cobweb down so firmly that Rowan yelped.

"You're insufferable," she said.

"And yet you can't keep away," Rowan said. She got to her feet, flashing Marion another wicked grin.

For a moment, Marion's face softened and Rowan thought she might smile back. Instead, she looked away, clearing her throat noisily.

"That should hold it for now," she said. "I don't think its deep enough for stitches, but you should get your friend Willow to have a look at it anyway. I dare say she knows more about all of this then I do."

Rowan nodded, bending to pick up her tunic. "You should come back with me," she said as she pulled it on. "This is our biggest take so far. There'll be celebrations tonight and you should be there. You've risked so much for us."

Marion shook her head. "They won't want me there. Your friends don't like nobles." She tried to hide the hurt from her voice, but Rowan knew her too well for that.

"That's only because they don't know you as I do," Rowan said. She hesitated for a moment, then laid her hand on Marion's arm. "Please, Marion, come back with me. Just for tonight."

Marion held her gaze and for a single, heart-soaring moment, Rowan thought she'd say yes. Then she shrugged the hand away, stared down at her feet.

"My father will be expecting me back," she mumbled. "I'll see you the day after tomorrow, as we agreed."

She looked up, met Rowan's eyes once more. "Go easy until that wound heals," she said. "I'll see you soon."

She turned and headed off into the trees. Rowan watched her go, feeling something tear deep inside her. With a sigh, she turned away and began the long walk back to camp.

✤ ✤ ✤

That night, the trees rang with the outlaw's celebrations. Alan had nabbed a couple of skins of mead from a tavern as they had fled through the town and now their faces were flushed and gleaming. Their laughter spilled over as Rowan told her side of the story and they imagined Gisborne limping back to tell his master that he had failed, the look on the sheriff's face when he found the money missing. The chest of stolen coins glinted liquid and buttery in the flickering firelight. They had plans to distribute it in a few days, once all the fuss had died down. The gold glittered in the other's eyes, the bright spark of victory.

And yet, Rowan was untouched by it all. She laughed along with the others and took swigs of the mead, but couldn't seem to *feel* any of it.

When Alan was distracting everyone with an impression of Gisborne staggering about bow-legged, she slipped away to the edge of the clearing. The forest hissed and sighed like a slumbering sea. She stared up through a gap in the canopy at the stars blinking down from a sky the deep, dreamless indigo of Marion's eyes. A near-full moon smiled down benevolently. Rowan leaned against a tree, sighing deeply and not even knowing why.

"You OK?"

Rowan looked around to see June stood beside her. She didn't seem to be as intoxicated as the others. Her speech hardly slurred, her stance swayed only slightly. Behind her, Rowan could see the others were now engaged in a dance of some sort, hopping and spinning like mad imps around the fire.

"Your wound troubling you?" June asked, gesturing

to Rowan's collar. Willow had declared Marion's efforts "passable" before cleaning and dressing the cut properly. It still throbbed, dull and persistent, but bearable.

"Nah," Rowan replied. "Willow fixed it up good."

June nodded. "Someone else helped too, right?" she added, her eyes sparkling in a way Rowan hadn't seen before. "That noble girl of yours."

"She's not my…" Rowan began, but stopped herself. Her skin still tingled with the memory of Marion's touch. She couldn't deny the tug at her heart anymore, that pure sweet ache.

June's eyes still gleamed in a far too knowing way for Rowan's taste, but she didn't press the matter.

"Maybe she's not so bad then," June said with a sniff, staring up at the stars.

Rowan smiled. "High praise indeed."

June gave a grunt that was almost a laugh.

They watched the others in silence. Alan had his head thrown back in song while the other two danced as if they were at a ball, bobbing and twirling and almost falling over. For once, they looked like any other group of teenagers, giddy with stolen wine and heady triumph.

"Fools," June said fondly, as Willow spun Mathew so wildly that he knocked into Alan, sending them both collapsing in a giggling heap to the forest floor.

"Yeah," Rowan agreed. "But I reckon they've earned a little foolishness."

"As have you," June said. She handed Rowan one of the skins of mead, now more than two thirds gone.

Rowan took it with a grin and June raised the second.

"To foolishness," Rowan said, knocking her own skin against June's.

"To friendship," June replied.

Rowan took a long gulp of honey wine. It lit a fire in her belly that spread down to her toes, lending the world a pleasant, warm fuzz.

June clapped her on the back and together they headed back to the welcome embrace of the fire.

CHAPTER THIRTEEN

Rowan woke with a jolt and instantly wished she hadn't. Her head was pounding, her body sore from yesterday's fight and then a night sleeping on the forest floor. She groaned and tried shutting her eyes again. But the pounding in her skull wouldn't let up. If anything, it was getting louder, a low rhythmic baying, almost like….

She sat bolt upright, her heart growing spikes. *Dogs.* The frantic barking of hunting hounds. And now she could make out the shouts interlaced with the baying. Far off but getting closer. And it was all too clear what their prey was.

Rowan scrambled to her feet and rushed to wake the others. She was met with groans and protests. Alan pulled his cloak full over his head.

"Come on!" Rowan snapped. "There are guards coming with dogs. We have to move, now."

June, who had been sitting up slowly, rubbing at her forehead, looked up, her eyes sharp. "How did they find us?"

"I don't know, I..."

Rowan's hand flew to her scarf, feeling its ragged end. Horror crept on spider feet up her spine. She had thought that Gisborne had merely torn it in the fight, but if he had ripped away a piece, even a small one, it would have enough of her scent for the dogs to find her. To find them all. She felt the snare tighten around her neck.

The others were moving quickly now, terror cutting through the sludge of sleep and last night's wine. Earth was kicked over the remains of the fire. Boots were pulled on, bows shouldered, the cloaks they had been sleeping under bundled up.

"Wait!" Rowan threw up a hand as they prepared to flee. "We should split up, confuse the scent trail."

She turned to Mathew and Alan. "You two head west."

It made sense for the boys to stick together. Mathew sometimes struggled to find his way in the forest and Alan was used to helping him. The two boys each took an end of the chest of prize money to carry between them. It would slow them down, but the idea of leaving behind what they had risked so much for was unbearable.

"Willow, you go north. I'll head east and June..."

"I'm coming with you," the bigger girl grunted. "You might need the back-up."

There was no time to argue, the baying of the dogs was getting louder.

"OK," Rowan nodded. "we'll meet at around midday, up by that cave we're using for winter stores.

Now, go!"

Without another word, the outlaws scattered like wind spun leaves.

* * *

Rowan and June ran for as long as they could. Rowan was naturally faster but she forced herself to match June's pace. Leaving the other girl behind to be torn apart was unthinkable. Even so, she tried not to let the bite of frustration show.

All morning, they darted through the trees, crashing through thickets, leaping fallen logs. They kept away from the main paths, which the guards were more likely to be using, cutting instead through waist high bracken, tripping on snarls of brambles.

Rowan splashed through every stream she saw, hoping to muddle the scent trail further. Soon she was soaked to the knees, her feet blistering in wet boots. Yet still she ran.

At long last, the sound of pursuit faded away entirely. Rowan slumped against a tree, unable to go another step. June sunk to her knees at the tree's roots, leaning back against the trunk, breathing heavily.

"I think we lost them," Rowan said when she finally had the breath to speak. She had pulled her mask and scarf over her face while they ran, in case one of the guards spotted them. Now she pushed them back, letting the gentle breeze cool the sweat on her skin.

June nodded, too spent for words.

For a few moments, they stood and sat in silence, catching their breath and listening to the forest. Rowan heard the song of a blackbird, the sigh of branches, the rustlings of a squirrel rummaging through the leaf litter. Familiar, safe sounds. No dogs. No guards. The tightness in her throat eased a little.

"C'mon," she said, pushing herself up off the tree trunk. She glanced up at the sky. "It's gone midday. We should go meet the others."

June nodded again. Rowan helped her to the feet, pulling her mask and scarf back in place. Together they picked their way through a tight thicket of saplings, stepping out onto a deer trail that ran alongside a steep rise in the forest floor.

Rowan turned slowly, trying to work out where they were. She froze. Ten paces away, an armoured guard stood in the centre of the path.

For a heartbeat, they just stared, each as surprised as the other. Then the man burst into action, one hand reaching for his sword, the other wrestling a hunting horn free from his belt. Before he could raise it to his lips, Rowan had her bow loaded and drawn, loosing the arrow all in one breath.

It skewered the man through the palm of his reaching hand. He dropped to his knees with a scream. But that was enough. Already Rowan could hear the sounds of men and horses further along the trail, the shouts and cantering hooves as they drew closer.

She grabbed June by the shoulder, shaking the other girl free of her shock. Together they turned and pelted into the trees.

CHAPTER FOURTEEN

They sprinted up the rise, away from the trail, the shouts of men and thunder of hooves chasing after them, arrows striking the ground at their heels. As they made the peak, June fell back with a howl, a feathered shaft protruding from her calf.

Rowan darted to her side at once, snapping away the arrow's shaft, wrapping June's scarf around the wound to stop the bleeding.

The other girl's face was chalk white. Sweat stood out big as raindrops on her skin. Her jaw was clenched and Rowan could feel her shaking.

Rowan felt her stomach constrict. This was her fault. If she hadn't baited the Sheriff, humiliated Gisborne, none of this would have happened. Marion had been right. This had all been a stupid, pointless risk, and now…

She could hear the men panting and huffing up the rise, heavy and slow in their armour. They had just moments before the guards were upon them. And now June couldn't run.

Rowan's eyes found an ancient oak, as gnarled and bent as an old man. Its trunk was hollow.

"Come on," she said, pulling June upright. "We'll hide you here, and I'll draw them away."

"No," June moaned as too much weight was put on her wounded leg. "You run, get away…"

"No chance," Rowan said, taking June's arm across her shoulders. "Once I've lost them, I'll double back and come fetch you. It'll be fine, I promise."

June started to protest, then she lost the will. Grey-faced, leaning on her axe for support, she allowed Rowan to conceal her in the tree.

"Stay down," Rowan breathed. "I'll be back soon."

She could hear the men's shouts growing closer. They had almost reached the top of the rise. Pausing only to kick fallen leaves over the blood trail June's tree, she took off, fast as a hawk through the trees. She heard the men's shouts as they spotted her. Her heart leapt in triumph then clutched in terror. Her plan had worked. Now what?

The ground shuddered with the horses' hooves. Even with her head start, Rowan knew she couldn't outrun horses, and the forest was too open here to lose them in the undergrowth. But the guards couldn't climb in their heavy armour.

She spotted another oak, this once huge and knotted, its upper branches thick and spreading.

She scrambled up the trunk nimble as a squirrel, her fingers finding cracks and knots in the bark, her boots scrabbling for purchase in their wake. She was careful to avoid the lower branches, which were rotten and didn't look like they would take her weight.

Bracing her toes against the bark, she straightened

her body out as far as it would go, reaching and leaping for the sturdy branch above her.

Both hands closed over it and she hung there, feet dangling, tried to pull herself up.

An arrow thudded into the wood just a breath from her hand. She snatched it away on impulse, crying out as her full weight shifted to one arm. She tried to reach back up, her muscles screaming, her fingers clawing bark.

Her grip failed and she hit the branch below with bruising force. She latched onto it with her arms and legs, heart booming, breath sawing, hands slippery with sweat.

She realised too late that the branch was one of the rotten ones. With a terrible crack, it gave way.

Rowan hit the forest floor with a bone-shaking thud. For a second her vision went black. Next thing she knew there were hands on her, hard fingers closing around her arms, knees pinning her legs. She tried to fight them off, but there were too many and her head still spun from the fall.

Her hands were bound behind her. She was forced to her feet.

She ached all over. Her mask and hood were still in place, though that couldn't last long. Fear was thrashing inside her. What would happen when they found out who she was, *what* she was?

One of the men reached out to pull the mask away, but another stopped him. "No," he barked. "We're to take him to the castle. The Sheriff wants to deal with this one himself."

CHAPTER FIFTEEN

They reached Nottingham as the sun was sinking behind the castle towers, turning the sky the fiery red of an infected wound. They had bound Rowan hand and foot and bundled her onto the back of one of the horses. Now they hurled her to the ground in the courtyard before the castle, cut her feet free and marched her through the huge oak doors.

Inside the castle was cold and shadowy, barely lit by the jumping light of torches. It smelt of tallow and smoke and bodies pressed together. People passed them, servants hurrying on errands, soldiers striding purposefully, lords in overladen finery. Some stopped to stare at Rowan, bound and hooded, marched along between the three guards. Others ignored her. Maybe doomed prisoners were an all too familiar sight in the castle these days.

Rowan hadn't been inside a stone building since she and her parents had left Locksley Manor house and she had forgotten how little she liked it. The cold walls seemed to be closing in, tightening around her chest. Her heart rattled against her ribs like a trapped bird. She wondered if she would ever see the forest again.

She was taken to a room in one of the towers, lit only by a couple of fretful candles. Two guards stayed with her, while the other left without a word. He returned soon enough, with the Sheriff of Nottingham in tow.

It was the first time Rowan had gotten a proper look at the man who had been her nemesis for the last three months. He was unremarkable, not particularly tall or finely dressed. His hair was mousy brown, his beard neatly trimmed. Only his eyes, cold and grasping as winter pools, betrayed his true nature. They lit up as soon as he saw Rowan, bound and helpless before him.

"We brought him to you for the unmasking as you ordered, my lord," one of the guards said.

"Indeed," the Sheriff said, his gaze travelling over Rowan's slight frame and shabby clothes, mouth twisted in disdain. "Come then, let's not wait any longer."

Rowan's hood was pulled back, revealing her long braid of reddish-brown hair. Her mask was torn away, the scarf lowered. She stared straight into the Sheriff's cold eyes and saw a smile spread slow as pond slime up his pale face.

"Well," he said. "You're not what I was expecting at all. What's your name, girl?"

Rowan's face slid into a smirk. "Why don't you buy me a drink first?"

A guard's fist cracked across her cheekbone. She staggered sideways. Another blow slammed into her stomach. She dropped to her knees, gasping for air, blood thundering in her skull.

She heard the Sheriff step towards her. His breath brushed her skin as he bent to murmur in her ear.

"I will ask you once more. Pray I do not have to do so a third time. Who are you?"

"Her name is Rowan Fletcher."

The voice came from the doorway. A bored, easy drawl that sent cold shivers through Rowan's guts.

She looked up. Guy of Gisborne leaned against the doorway. He was smiling at her in a way that made her skin crawl.

"She's from Locksley," he went on. "She's no one, a nothing. After she attacked me, I sought out those who had known her in the village, looking for a family to take punishment in her place. But there was no one. Her father was hanged for a thief last year, her mother's dead too. She's alone in the world."

Gisborne barked a laugh as he stepped into the room. "When I heard you had caught the Green Hood," he said. "I wanted to see him for myself. I had no idea it would be someone so... disappointing."

His eye roamed over Rowan. She forced herself not to flinch.

"Ah," said the Sheriff, glancing from one to the other. "*This* is the wild cat who clawed out your eye?"

Rage crossed Gisborne's face, but he nodded all the same.

"What a small world it is!"

The sheriff stepped forward, crouched down so his face was on a level with Rowan's.

"Well, my little wild cat, you're not alone anymore, are you?" His voice was calm and soft, almost gentle. His face would have been amicable, if not for the frost burning behind his eyes.

"Yesterday, you and that band of miscreants you run with stole a great deal of money from me. Tell me where it is, tell me the names of those who stole it with you, and I might even spare your life."

Rowan could feel half of her face swelling up. Even so, she slipped her sideways smile back in place.

"Afraid I spent it already. Terrible gambling habit, you know."

The sheriff sighed, as if deeply disappointed. He straightened up and turned away.

A mailed fist crunched into Rowan's jaw, knocking her sprawling. Her lip burst open. She choked on blood. They hauled her up into a chair, looping her bound hands over the back.

"We'll hang her at dawn," came the Sheriff's voice, warping and wavering through the clanging in her head. "Until then, get what you can out of her. I don't care how you do it."

"Leave her to me," Gisborne said. His smile was a skull's, all teeth and hunger. "I'll make her talk, believe me."

The Sheriff shook his head. "Come back at midnight, Guy. Let them soften up the meat first. If she hasn't talked by then, you have my permission to do as you wish."

He looked back at Rowan, his eyes gleaming. "After all, the anticipation will make it all the sweeter."

With that, the Sheriff and Gisborne left Rowan alone with the guards and their unforgiving fists.

CHAPTER SIXTEEN

Marion was in her room, lighting her candles for the night, when she heard a soft tap at her window. She froze, straining to listen, thinking she might have imagined it. It came again, a small plip dropped into the silence of the night.

Marion crossed to the window, pushed back the shutters and leaned out into the mild summer air. The full moon smiled down at her, and by its light, she could just make out two figures standing beneath her window. One had hair as pale as starlight on snow. His upturned face was beseeching. The other was darker, scowling, his jaw clenched in worry.

Marion recognised their clothes if not their faces. These two had been among the outlaws who held her up on the North Road. They were part of Rowan's gang.

"Lady Marion," said the paler boy. "We met the other day. My name's Mathew and this is Alan."

"What are you doing here?" Marion hissed, leaning out as far as she dared. "If someone sees you, it could ruin everything!"

They were lucky that her room was at the back of the house, facing the woods. If a servant, or worse her father, saw the two boys, then questions would be asked. Marion's heart stuttered at the thought.

"I'm sorry, my lady," said Mathew. "But we had to come."

"Why?" Marion asked, feeling her stomach clench. "What's happened?"

"It's Rowan," said Alan. "She's been captured."

Captured! The word cut sharp as frost through the warm night. Marion stared at them in horror.

"When? How?"

"Earlier today," Mathew said. "The sheriff sent guards after us with hunting dogs. We split up and agreed to meet up later, but Rowan and June never arrived. We found June later, in a hollow tree. She was injured, shot in the leg. She said that Rowan had tried to lead the guards away from her and gotten caught."

Mathew swallowed. "We think they've taken her to the castle."

Marion saw Rowan dashing through the forest, desperate to escape the pursuing guards. She saw her chained in some foul castle dungeon. She saw her bound and hooded, approaching the hangman's noose.

Marion's stomach turned over. She forced the nausea down with several long, steadying breaths before looking back at the boys.

Mathew was still staring up at her, his eyes round and pleading. "Please, my lady," he begged. "We came to you because we think you're the only one with any chance of getting her out. None of us could even get into the castle, but you could just walk through the front door. Please, say you'll at least try."

Marion thought of Gisborne, with his leering gaze and too-friendly hands. She thought of the Sheriff, with his cold, flat eyes and careful sneer. What would they do to Marion if they caught her rescuing a prisoner? She dared not think. But the thought of Rowan in the castle, alone and frightened, facing certain death, was far worse.

"Alright," she said. "I will try."

***

"I'm just saying, I don't see why Gisborne should get all the fun."

"Shut up, you fool."

"What, can he hear through solid walls now?"

"You've heard the stories about him."

"So what? I'm not afraid of him."

"You should be."

Rowan, slumped in her bonds, barely registered the guard's conversation. Blood dribbled off her nose and dropped to a puddle on the floor. She watched the ripples with a dull kind of fascination.

Her chest was full of broken shards. They grated against each other with every breath. Her face was swollen and felt not remotely like her own anymore. She had long since lost the strength to scream.

"Look, we've still got a bit of time before he turns up. Long enough for me to have a go at any rate."

"Don't be an idiot. If Gisborne's marked the girl as his, you'd be stupid to defy him."

"He'll never even know…"

It was only then that Rowan realised what they were talking about. The spike of fear flooded her with enough adrenaline to come to her senses. She primed her muscles, ready to fight back in whatever way she could. What she could do when she was bound and beaten half to death, she didn't know.

There was a knock at the door. Rowan's terror

spiked higher, thinking it was Gisborne come early. Clearly so did the guards, for they both jumped, turning to the door. But when it opened, someone quite different stepped into the tiny room.

A guard gasped. "Lady Marion!"

Just the name was enough to flood Rowan's body with hope. As her blood-blurred vision cleared, she could make out Marion stood in the doorway. She wore a dark cloak, her curls windswept, her face fiercely defiant.

"I insist that you give me some time alone with this prisoner," she told the guards, her voice at its most haughtily authoritative.

The guards looked awkward. "I'm sorry, my lady, but we've been ordered by the Sheriff to stay until midnight."

Marion turned her hawk-like glare on the man who had spoken. "My cousin is the King. His authority outranks that of the Sheriff by quite a margin. I demand that you leave this room *at once* or I will tell him of your insolence."

The two guards looked at each other, weighing up the wrath of their master against that of this young woman. Eventually, they seemed to decide that she meant what she said and left the room without a word, locking the door behind them.

Marion rushed over and dropped to her knees before the chair. Rowan felt gentle hands on her shoulders, her face, lifting it up. She heard Marion gasp in horror.

"Merciful Saints, what have they done to you?"

"Trust me, I've looked worse." The words tasted rusty. Her attempted smile fell sideways and swung loose.

She tried her best to hide how much even Marion's gentle touch hurt. It was worth it just to see her again, to hear her voice and breathe her sweet, clean scent.

"We need to get you out of here," Marion said, her voice hurried, her eyes casting around for a way out. She drew the small knife from inside her cloak, the same one she had held Rowan hostage with on her first day back in Nottingham. "I'll cut you loose, then scream to draw the guards. When they come in, we'll knock them out, and then…"

"No. We can't. It's too risky. You'll only get caught too, and I need you free. I need you alive."

Rowan swallowed, tasted blood and bile. "Go to the forest. Find the others. Tell them to run, to hide somewhere even I don't know about. Tell them to take their families too, because… Gisborne's coming and I don't know… I don't think I can last… not against him and I don't want… I can't get them hurt too…"

Her words ended in a choked sob. Marion's hand tightened on her arm. In the low light, Rowan could see that her eyes were bright with tears.

"I can't," Marion whispered. "I can't leave you here to die."

"You must. You think I could live with myself if my escape got you killed? The most painful death in the world is preferable to that."

Far away, a bell tolled out twelve times. Marion's head jerked towards the sound. When she looked back at Rowan, her eyes were wide and scared.

"Leave me the knife," said Rowan. "Let me go down fighting at least. If I make it out of here, I'll see you again. I swear."

The ring of footsteps outside, approaching the

chamber. Marion looked at her for the longest moment. Then, as the footsteps were replaced with the sound of Gisborne arguing with the guards stationed outside the chamber, Marion leaned in close.

Her lips met Rowan's own, and there was a moment of such perfect bliss Rowan's head swam with it. Marion's lips tasted just as Rowan remembered, soft and sweet. She could smell Marion's clean, perfumed skin, the night air clinging to her clothes.

Far too soon, she drew away. Rowan could see the smallest smudge of blood on Marion's lips. Her own, she realised.

"I love you," said Marion. She slipped the knife into Rowan's bound hands. She brushed a hand across her lips, then straightened and turned back to the door as it swung open.

Gisborne strode into the room, handsome face ugly with rage. The sight of Marion pulled him up short.

"Lady Marion," he said, eyebrows raised. "This is an unexpected pleasure."

Marion stood straight and tall, her expression ferocious as she glared the man down. "I wanted to make sure your brutes didn't kill this poor girl."

"Your compassion is admirable, my lady, but I fear it is wasted on this wretch."

Marion refused to back down. "The treatment of this prisoner has been abominable! I demand that she be given a fair trial."

Gisborne laughed incredulously. "My lady, this girl is a dangerous criminal, and she will be treated accordingly. An example must be made of rabble-rousers or we'll have a revolt on our hands."

Marion continued to glare with all the sharp pride

of a bird of prey. "I can assure you, Sir Guy, the King will hear of this brutality."

"By all means, you must act as you feel is best," Gisborne said with an exaggerated bow. It was clear he didn't think the King would take much interest in the abuse of one peasant girl. Even if he did, Rowan would be dead long before the King could offer any kind of reprisal.

"Now, I must insist you leave, my lady," Gisborne went on, straightening up, a dark eagerness in his voice. "I fear that our interrogation methods may be too much for your... delicate sensitivities."

Marion still seemed reluctant. She chanced a glance back at Rowan, who gave her the smallest of nods, unseen by Gisborne. Marion threw the man a final contemptuous glare and swept from the room.

Gisborne shut the door behind her. There was a click as the guards locked it on the other side. He turned to Rowan, striding across the room, his face furious.

"You little bitch," he snarled, back-handing her across the face. Her head snapped sideways, blood spraying from her lips.

The jolt nearly knocked the knife from her grip, but she managed to keep hold of it. Rowan had been sawing through her bonds throughout Marion and Gisborne's conversation. The knife blade was small and the rope thick, but she was making progress.

"What did you tell her, eh?" Gisborne yanked her face around to look at him, his fingers bruisingly tight on her chin. "What lies have you been feeding her?"

Rowan said nothing. Gisborne's hand went to his belt. It came back clutching a dagger. He rested it against her cheekbone, right beneath her right eye, pressing the blade in hard enough to make tears of blood weep down her face and drip off her chin.

"Here's what's going to happen," he said, voice soft as a simmering flame. "You're going to tell me the names and locations of those vagabonds you call friends. If you don't, I'll slice off your fingers one by one. You will never hold a bow again. I will cut you away, piece by piece. Now, speak!"

Rowan still made no reply. She was almost through the rope now.

Gisborne yanked her head back by the hair. He moved his dagger to Rowan's hairline, digging the tip in until the blood welled.

"I'm going to give you to the count of three," Gisborne breathed, his face so close to hers that his silken whisper chilled her skin. "Or I will repay you the favour you did me. An eye for an eye, as the bible says." He dragged the knife down slowly towards her eyebrow, his smile savouring the taste of her pain.

Rowan clenched her teeth against the cry tearing at her throat. She forced all her attention on those last few strands of rope, on the thin blade sawing her way to freedom.

"One…"

Rowan's sweat-slicked hands shook, her scrambling fingers fought to keep their grip on the knife.

"Two…"

Hot blood stung her eyes. Her vision filled with swimming red.

"Three."

The rope snapped. Rowan swung her arm around and sunk the blade deep into Gisborne's throat.

Gisborne's grip went slack. The dagger fell away with a clatter. His enraged eye clouded with surprise. His hands reached for his neck and Rowan ripped the knife free in a billow of scarlet. Blood spattered her skin, warm as summer rain.

Gisborne's mouth worked as he tried to scream, tried to breathe. Nothing but a wet bubbling escaped his lips. His body slipped sideways, and he fell face down into a rising sea of red.

Rowan staggered to her feet and scrambled to the far side of the room, away from the body. She was breathing heavily, and the hand grasping the knife was slippery and shaking. She thrust the weapon into her belt, dragged a sleeve across her eyes to clear away the blood.

Her every bone was screaming for rest, but she knew she couldn't remain still for a moment. She had to get out of here before the guards came back.

She could check if Gisborne had a key for the door on him, but the idea of approaching, never mind touching the body, was too sickening for words. Anyway, there were still guards posted outside and she was in no state to fight them.

She staggered to the window, pulling back the shutters. She looked down at the castle courtyard, bathed with moonlight. She could see that the front gates were closed and could make out guards patrolling the ramparts.

Glancing down, she saw the walkway that ran along the wall circling the courtyard passed beneath her window. She had dropped further from trees many times before, but with her whole body on fire, her spirit quailed at the thought.

Taking a fortifying breath of cool night air, she clambered onto the windowsill. Telling herself that she was on a branch above the soft forest floor, she stepped to the edge and let herself fall.

Her whole being screeched with the impact. Biting off the cry, she curled into a tight ball, rolling over and over until she came to rest in a small, shuddering huddle. She crushed her face into the stone to muffle the sobs.

When she could breathe easily again, she looked up. No one had seen her. The nearest guard patrol seemed far away.

Body bent in a crouch, she crept to the edge of the castle wall, keeping to the shadows. She needed to find a way down into the town below, but that wasn't easy when there was no cover.

As carefully and quickly as she could, she slipped along the wall, peering over the edge for a suitable spot. At last, she saw it a little way ahead. The thatched roof of a house built against the castle wall.

She heard rumbling voices behind her and froze. Another guard patrol, approaching fast. She could hear their clunking footsteps, the rattle of their armour. Any second now, they would round the bend in the wall and see her.

Heart thudding, she sprinted to the stretch of wall above the house and vaulted over the ramparts. This time the landing was easier. The thatch of the roof provided some cushioning. Even so, her ribs shrieked their protest as she slid down the roof and dropped to the street below. She stumbled to a gap between two houses and doubled up, breathing heavily, her senses straining for sounds of pursuit. None came.

She straightened and looked about, scanning the moon-paved road before her. She knew she wasn't safe yet. More guards patrolled the town at night, and even if she got past them unseen, it was a long walk back to the forest. Her legs shook at the thought. She barely had the strength to stand, let alone make such a perilous journey.

She thought of Marion's soft lips and whispered words. She touched a hand to the knife in her belt. She straightened her spine, sheathed her insides in steel. She had to do this. She had to survive. She had too much to live for.

Taking her courage in her teeth, she stepped out into the night.

CHAPTER SEVENTEEN

Grey morning light was streaming through the castle windows as the Sheriff made his way up to the tower room. He forced himself to keep his face calm, to not show the anticipating bubbling inside him.

Gisborne would have had the girl for almost six hours now. He was most accomplished at this kind of task. The Sheriff looked forward to seeing what Gisborne had done to the prisoner.

He remembered how the girl had looked at him the previous evening, the defiance curling her lip and blazing in her eyes. He felt anger constrict his insides. He hoped Gisborne had smashed that look from her face.

He reached the door to the prisoner's cell, and the one of the guards unlocked it for him. He entered the room.

The first thing that struck him was the stench of blood, the iron tang that crawled down your throat and made your gorge rise.

His eyes fell on the empty chair. His gaze continued down, settling on something sprawled on the floor. Black leather, crusted blood, flies buzzing around a staring eye.

Behind him, one of the guards gasped. The other made a retching sound. The Sheriff made no noise at all. No movement, no reaction, not the nearest flicker of emotion crossed his face.

From the waxy pallor of Gisborne's skin, the stiffness of his limbs and the claggy consistency of the blood, the Sheriff could tell he had been there a while. He could make out a wound on his neck, a wide ragged hole.

The Sheriff let the cold rage wrap itself around him like armour, let it sculpt his face into a mask of ice.

"What happened?" he said, not looking up from the corpse. The guards flinched from the calm fury in his voice.

The guards started to stammer that they had done as he instructed, worked on the girl until midnight, then Sir Guy had come in to take over, and no one had entered or exited the room since he had.

The Sheriff peered closer at the wound on Gisborne's neck. Made by a knife, he decided. But the girl didn't have a knife. She had been searched thoroughly and all her weapons removed. Unless…

"Did anyone else enter this room?" the Sheriff asked, his voice quick and cutting. "Before Gisborne did?"

He saw the guards shoot a look at each other, felt their reluctance burning on the air.

"Speak! Who else came in here?"

"Lady Marion," one of the guard's said, eyes downcast. "She came in a little before midnight, demanded to be left alone with the prisoner. But she wasn't in there long, certainly not long enough to…" He trailed off, seeming to realise what he was saying.

Fools, the Sheriff thought. He'd have both their

heads for this. Even so, their answer surprised him. Lady Marion? What interest did she have in any of this? Then again, her father had once been Lord of Locksley, where the outlaw girl was from. Could they have met then, formed some sort of friendship? But what would a noblewoman like Marion want with a scruffy peasant girl?

The Sheriff stared out the window to the rain-soaked sky beyond, thinking. In theory, Lady Marion's status as the King's cousin made her untouchable. But the King was far away, preoccupied with his war, and his brother was much more sympathetic to the Sheriff's needs. It was the prince who had had d'Aubigny instated as Sheriff of Nottingham in the first place. Surely, he would understand.

"Send a troop of guards to Wolfstone Manor," he told the guards. "Bring Lord Fordwin and Lady Marion back to the castle immediately."

He stared back at Gisborne's corpse, his lip curling in disgust. Idiot, to have been bested by a peasant girl, not once but twice. The Sheriff was glad to be rid of him. "And send someone to clear up this mess."

CHAPTER EIGHTEEN

Rain was tapping a ponderous heartbeat against the forest canopy as Mathew and Alan walked side by side through the dripping trees. The air was rich with the scent of damp earth and wet leaves.

The sun was barely up before the two boys had headed out of camp, searching the forest for Rowan. They walked with heavy hearts, sodden with rain and worry. They knew how slim the chances were of Rowan getting out of the castle, slimmer still that she would make it back to them alive.

Yet they couldn't sit and wait any longer, so they gone out to look for her. Mathew's hope was that, if Rowan had got out, she would be heading for the cave too, their decided rendezvous from the previous day. Their best bet was to walk in a tight spiral through the woods around the cave and hope that they found her.

June had stayed behind, resting her injured leg and Willow had stayed with her in case the wound needed further attention.

The previous night had been the longest of

Mathew's life. When June and Rowan hadn't arrived at the cave, Alan went looking for them. He found June hidden in a hollow tree, clutching her injured leg and babbling about Rowan being captured. The guards who took her had ridden straight past June with Rowan bound and helpless among them, too fast for June to do anything. She had been grey-faced and half-delirious.

Willow at once took over tending to her wound while the boys looked at each other, scrambling for something to do. In the end, they did the only thing they could and went to find Marion.

After the noblewoman had promised to help, the boys had little choice but to return to camp and wait. Mathew sat up by the fire, longing for dawn yet dreading it all the same. Beside him June groaned and thrashed in her sleep, her wounded leg making her restless no matter what Willow gave her.

The others tried to sleep but Mathew sensed they were awake in the dark around him, waiting for the sun to show its face. He wondered if, like him, they were thinking about what Rowan might be going through at the hands of Gisborne and the Sheriff. He wondered if the idea made them feel as sick as he did.

The stolen chest had squatted like a fat little goblin in one corner of the cave. Mathew couldn't bring himself to look at it, the cost of obtaining it suddenly much too high.

Alan walked beside him, his face pale, his eyes dark and tired. He had barely spoken a word since they had returned the previous night. It was strange to see him so subdued. He was so unlike the Alan from the night after the archery contest, singing and laughing and flushed with triumph. It was as if that boy didn't exist anymore.

Mathew had known Rowan a long time but it was only last night that he realised how close the others had grown to her over the last few months. They were as desperate to have her back as he was. He stared out across the rain-washed forest, remembering a dozen other morning walks he had gone on with Rowan back before they were outlaws.

He tripped over something. It groaned. He looked down, startled. It was Rowan!

If it wasn't for the dyed-green tunic with its stitched-on hood, Mathew may not have recognised his best friend. She was curled on her side, both arms wrapped around her ribs. Her face was swollen with bruises and crusted with blood. Her clothes were filthy and rumpled, soaked through with rain. Her braid was coming undone, her hair matted with grime.

Mathew could just make out the rise and fall of her chest. When he knelt beside her, he could feel the whisper of breath against his hand, the patter of a pulse in her neck.

He looked up at Alan and knew the other boy was thinking just the same as he was. They couldn't carry her by themselves and he was scared to try in case they hurt her more.

"I'll go get the others," Alan said and took off through the trees.

Mathew took Rowan's hand, limp and cold in his own. He felt the trapped butterfly flutterings of a pulse at her wrist. He could hear her breathing, slow and laboured, almost lost beneath the drumming of the rain.

"Just hold on," he said under his breath. "Just a little longer, until the others get here. Just keep fighting."

After what felt like hours but was more like

minutes, he heard the scramble of Alan's footsteps running back through the trees. Mathew looked up and saw Willow running beside him, with June stomping along behind them, using her axe shaft as a crutch.

June took one look at Rowan and, ignoring Willow's protests about her leg, bent down and scooped the unconscious girl up as if she weighed nothing at all. Rowan gave the smallest moan as June draped her gently over her broad shoulders.

Batting away a fussing Willow and insisting she was fine, June straightened and using her axe for support, turned and made her awkward way back to camp.

* * *

For some weeks now, the outlaws had been searching for a more permanent place to settle. All summer they had moved around, sleeping in the open air and breaking camp often to avoid the search parties that the Sheriff sent out to find them. But summer was already losing its battle with autumn. Blackberries baked in the midday sun, filling the forest with sweetness. Early morning mists had begun to sweep in. Winter would soon follow, and they needed to find somewhere more sheltered.

A few days ago, Willow had found just such a place. A small opening at the base of a sandstone rock face, which after a short drop down opened into a rounded cave, about the same size as the cottage Willow had once shared with her mother and brother.

She had shown it to the others and they had been using it for storage, with the plan of moving in more permanently after the archery contest. They had found a small opening in the ceiling to use as a smoke hole and woven a screen out of bracken and fallen branches to cover the opening.

Once they'd found June in the hollow tree, it had taken all three of them to get her back to the cave. Now it was here that they took Rowan.

June dropped through the opening and laid Rowan down as gently as she could on the nearest bed roll. Then she collapsed by the fire, cradling her leg, face grey and slicked with sweat. Willow jumped down after her and knelt by Rowan's side.

Her mother's lessons in herblore spun around her head. Faced with Rowan's injuries, they felt woefully inadequate. Still, she was the best chance Rowan had, so she bent her head over her friend's body and set to work.

"I think her ribs are broken," she said after a quick examination. "I'll do what I can, but if she's bleeding inside..." She couldn't face putting it into words.

If the ribs were broken, there was little to be done except leave them to heal. Willow brewed an infusion for the pain out of crushed poppy seeds and poured it between Rowan's lips. She mixed poultices and smeared them over the cuts and bruises across her face and torso to fight off infection and reduce the swelling. She cleaned the wound on Rowan's forehead and stuck it shut with cobwebs. She had the others boil up a strengthening broth from deer bones and fed it to Rowan in spoonfuls while Mathew held her head tilted upward.

Through it all, Rowan didn't so much as twitch. And through it all, Willow had to fight the screaming voice in her head that it was too late, it was all for nothing, that Rowan was dying and nothing she did would make any difference.

June sat watching from the other side of the fire, her face ashen even though Willow had changed the dressing on her leg and given her willow bark to chew. Alan paced the small space, restless with fear. Mathew crouched by Rowan's side, her hand in his. His eyes were huge, his face so pale he looked carved from chalk.

All morning, they watched Rowan's chest rise and fall, as if it were their will alone that kept her breathing. Sometimes she lay still as the dead. Around midmorning, she began to twitch and moan as the pain tore through her. She called out in her sleep, for her mother, her father. For Marion.

By midday, Alan couldn't stand the tension any longer and announced he was going hunting. Willow didn't try to stop him. She did what she could to keep herself busy, grinding herbs, mixing medicines, anything that would stop her fixating on that tiny beat of a pulse in Rowan's neck. It seemed to get fainter every time she checked.

Come back, she begged silently. *Please, please come back. We need you, all of Nottingham needs you. Please, come back to us.*

CHAPTER NINETEEN

The forest looked different in the rain, dark and disorientating. Marion had been wandering for hours and she was thoroughly lost. She had ridden to the point on the North Road where she thought she had first encountered the outlaws. Then, leaving her horse tethered, she set off into the forest on foot. She had been making the bird call Rowan taught her, hooting like an owl in the light of day. But it hadn't worked yet, and she was growing scared it never would.

Her wool cloak grew sodden with rain, clinging to her as heavy as her dread. She hadn't dared return to the castle that morning in case it looked suspicious. She had no idea if Rowan had escaped, if she was even alive.

Please be alive. Please be safe. Please, please, please don't leave me.

She heard a noise behind her and spun around, hand flying to the knife she normally kept at her belt before remembering that she gave it to Rowan. She froze, listening desperately.

At first nothing, just the rain drumming out the

forest's heartbeat. Then, there! A hooting owl. Marion hesitated for a moment, wondering what to do. Then, for lack of anything else, she made the call again.

Out of the shadows stepped a boy dressed in shades of brown and green. His chestnut hair clung to his scalp. A bow and quiver were slung over one shoulder, a brace of woodpigeons hanging from one hand. He lowered the scarf across his mouth and nose. Marion recognised Alan. His face was drawn and pale, his eyes ringed with dark. Clearly, he hadn't slept much either.

He blinked at her in surprise. "It's you," he said, perplexed. "I didn't think you would come."

"Is she alright?" she asked, voice tight and straining. "Is she alive?"

Alan nodded. Marion felt her whole being sag with relief.

"At least, she was when I left."

"Can I see her?" Marion didn't care how pleading her voice had become.

Alan looked at her for a few moments, considering her. Finally, he nodded. Without a word, he turned and set off through the trees, Marion hurrying to keep up.

❊ ❊ ❊

Alan led Marion to the cave. She jumped down after him. Once her eyes had adjusted to the low light, she found herself in a small, rounded space of warm yellow sandstone, with a fire at its centre. Four other people occupied the cave. One of them was lying very still.

Marion gave a gasp that was half shock, half relief when she saw Rowan lying in the cave's corner. She dropped to her side at once, clutching the hand that

Mathew wasn't already holding. She felt the pulse in Rowan's wrist, so faint, so frail. But still there, still alive.

She heard a scuffle behind her and turned to see June trying to get to her feet and slumping back again, her bandaged leg collapsing under her. She was staring at Alan in shocked outrage.

"What did you bring *her* here for?" she said to him. "What if she tells them where we are?"

Alan sighed as he slung off his bow and quiver and propped them against the cave wall. "I think she's more than proven her loyalty. She helped Rowan escape."

This seemed to silence June, but she still eyed Marion with suspicion. Her mistrust would have hurt, but there wasn't space in Marion to feel anything else. She couldn't tear her eyes away from Rowan's face.

The injuries had looked bad enough in the flickering dimness of the tower room, but by the light of the fire and the cave's opening, they were horrific. Her skin was stained every shade of blue and purple, her face so swollen she was almost unrecognisable. The outlaws had wrapped her in blankets, yet the hand Marion held still felt cold, clammy.

Hold on, my love. Please, don't leave me.

Across Rowan's body, Mathew caught Marion's eye and offered up a weak smile. "You got her out," he said. His voice was quiet, as if he could sense death lurking in the corners of the cave and feared drawing it closer. "Thank you."

Marion shook her head. She was startled to find she was swallowing back tears. "I didn't do anything," she choked out. "I just gave her a knife. The rest was all her."

"You mean this knife?" Mathew held up the small weapon, which had been lying beside the sleeping girl.

Marion recognised the pearl-inlaid hilt, the blade glinting wickedly sliver in the firelight.

"We found it on her," Mathew said. He offered it back to her hilt first.

Marion shook her head again. "She can keep it. She'll need it more than me."

It was a wrench to give up the little blade, which was her protection, her freedom. But she wanted Rowan to have something of hers. It would make her feel like she was close to her even when she wasn't. It was like a promise. Rowan could only use the knife if she woke up. Therefore, she had to wake up.

"Rowan told me that you knew each other growing up," June said. There was still a hard edge to her voice, but she was clearly trying to sound more reasonable. "That you were close."

Marion turned to look at her. The tall girl was sat by the fire, her face softer without the shards of suspicion in her eyes.

Alan sat beside her, his head bent over the pigeon he was plucking. The dark-haired girl, who Marion hadn't been properly introduced to, knelt by Rowan's head, mixing a poultice for her wounds, her long hair forming a curtain that obscured her face. Marion was certain they were both listening intently. Mathew was staring at her, eyes wide and pale as full moons.

She took a breath and nodded. She'd had enough of hiding who she was from everyone, even herself. These people had trusted her with their lives, their secrets. It seemed only fair that she should do the same.

"We were very close," she said, looking back at Rowan. "Much closer than friends." She ran a hand down the girl's face. She stirred slightly, murmuring something.

"But we had to keep it a secret," Marion went on. With each word, she felt as if she was releasing something within herself. "Or else they'd kill her, maybe even burn her alive. Me too, if it weren't for my father's protection. I think her parents knew, though they never seemed to mind. They were always happy to see me, proud to see us together…"

She trailed off, grief choking her words. She had only found out that Rowan's parents were dead days ago, and she still couldn't believe she would never bask in their warmth and kindness again. Marion had lost her own mother when she was too small to even remember her. Her father had always been distant, happy to let Marion be raised by an army of nannies and maidservants. In Rowan's parents, she had found the affection she had been so desperately craving as a child.

She sniffed and forced herself to carry on. "Some of the young lords at court seemed to suspect that I was different. They used to whisper that something must be 'wrong' with me, or how else could I resist their charms?"

She wrinkled her nose in disgust. "Swaggering, arrogant brats, every one of them. And Gisborne's worse. My father wants me to marry him so we can regain our lands. I think that might be why Gisborne petitioned the Sheriff to give him the land in the first place. I think he hoped to trap me into marrying him. My father's accepting my refusal for the time being, partly because he's still so angry at the pair of them, but who knows how long that'll last."

She gazed back down at Rowan's sleeping face. She felt something soften and strengthen inside her.

"But I don't care," she added, her voice lined in steel, edged with defiance. "She's the only person I've ever loved or ever will. And none of them can take that from me."

Silence followed these words. Marion sat and listened to Rowan's gentle breathing. She could feel the other girl's pulse keeping time with the rain outside, as if the forest lived within her, as if it were the only thing keeping her alive.

"She feels the same about you." Mathew's words were so unexpected in the silence that Marion gave a start. She looked at him. The boy's gaze was stark and solemn beneath his snow-white fringe.

"You can see it," he said. "It's in her eyes when she looks at you, in her voice when she speaks of you. She might not say it, but she feels it. I know she does."

Across the fire, June nodded slowly, her face all stony certainty. The other two remained silent, but there was a different quality to the silence than what Marion had experienced before. Not hostile, not fearful, not judging. For the first time in her life, Marion felt part of something. She felt accepted.

She smiled at Mathew, a smile that was all angles and swallowed tears, but she meant it.

"Thank you," she said.

The boy shrugged and looked back down at Rowan. The girl slept on, unknowing that, for Marion at least, everything had changed.

CHAPTER TWENTY

Evening was fuzzing the edges of the world by the time Marion returned to Wolfstone Manor. She thought it best to lay low at home for a couple of days, then maybe she could go back to the castle and collect more information for Rowan and the others. The thought of having a reason to go see the girl she loved again made her heart leap in cautious hope, like a baby bird testing its wings.

As she drew into the courtyard before the manor, she felt at once that something was wrong. The night was too still, too quiet. The windows of the manor were as dark as skulls' eyes. Why hadn't the servants lit the candles yet?

She dismounted cautiously, reaching for her knife, and then remembering she'd left it in the forest. She looked about her, that feeling of wrongness still prickling at the back of her neck. Where was everyone? Normally, John the stable boy would have run out to take her horse by now. Yet the courtyard was still, silent, dead…

"Lady Marion."

She had to bite back a cry. Spinning around, she saw a figure stepping out of the shadows. He was tall, strong, armoured. Though the nose guard of his helmet obscured his face, Marion still recognised him as the captain of the Sheriff's guardsmen. Fresh panic sunk its claws in.

She forced herself to stand tall, to look the man in the eye. "Good evening, captain," she said, throwing on her most imperious tone. "Might I ask why we have the pleasure of your company?"

Sweat prickled Marion's spine as more guards stepped out of the dark at the courtyard's edges, spreading out to surround her.

The captain's face was inscrutable. "I must ask you to come with us."

Marion glared while her insides quailed. "Why?"

"The Sheriff's orders."

He motioned two of his men forward, who seized Marion's arms on either side. She struggled, panic clawing higher in her throat.

"I demand to know what this is about," she said, trying to sound commanding rather than terrified. "Where is my father, our servants?"

"You are under arrest for suspected treason," the captain said, already turning away from her and striding back towards the courtyard's entrance, his men following. "I suggest you come quietly."

They left Marion's horse standing confused and alone in the courtyard as they dragged her towards where they'd left their own mounts. As she fought and struggled, Marion's mind screamed one question over and over. *How the hell did he find out?*

※ ※ ※

Rowan was adrift on a gentle sea. Then sharp rocks

scraped against her skin, boring up through her chest, lighting up her ribs with every breath. She struggled to stay asleep, reaching for it like a fallen blanket. But the pain in her ribs was only growing, and she came awake with a gasp.

She blinked and looked around. Her surroundings were unfamiliar, rounded walls of smooth, honey-coloured stone. Daylight was seeping through an opening, and through it she could hear bird song, leaf rustle, branches sighing. The sound of the forest. She breathed a sigh of relief. She was home.

She tried to sit up, only to collapse with a groan. Her ribs burned. Her head throbbed. Her limbs ached.

Mathew, crouched by the fire at the cave's centre, looked up at the noise. His face split into a grin so wide she thought his skin would crack.

"Thank God," he said, shuffling over to her. "We were beginning to think you'd never wake."

"How long...?" Rowan croaked; her voice parched from lack of use.

"A day and a night," said Mathew, passing her a water skin which she gulped from gratefully. "It's been... well, it's been touch and go. There were times when I thought..."

He looked away; his face pained. Rowan could see shadows underlining his eyes. She wondered how long it had been since he last slept.

She ran a hand through her sweat-damp hair. Twenty-four hours. The tower room, Gisborne's death, Marion's kiss. It all felt like so long ago.

"Marion!" she said with a start. "Is she alright? Did she get out OK?"

"She's fine," said Mathew. "She came to see you

yesterday."

Rowan felt the tightness in her chest ease. "Where are the others?"

Mathew jerked a thumb over his shoulder. Rowan peered past him and into the gloom at the back of the cave. She could just make out the slumbering forms of June and Willow.

"I made them get some sleep," said Mathew. "Willow's been working herself thin trying to care for you and tend June's leg. Alan went out to get supplies."

"You look like you could use some rest yourself," Rowan said, eyeing his worry-worn face.

Mathew gave her a tired smile. "I'll be OK. I wanted there to be someone with you when you woke up."

Rowan smiled back, a broken, pained thing that did nothing to sum up the depths of gratitude she felt for all of them.

Silence fell as Mathew went about hanging a pot of the previous night's stew over the fire.

Rowan tried, with more success this time, to sit up. She eased herself carefully against the cave wall. Pushing back the blanket, she saw that she was in just her shirt and leggings. Her tunic and boots were by the fire, now dry and warm.

Beneath the shirt, her damaged ribs grumbled their resentment. She felt her face gingerly, and while the bruises still smarted, the worst of the swelling seemed to have gone down. Willow clearly knew her stuff.

"Here." Mathew thrust a bowl of stew and a hunk of bread into her hands. "You haven't eaten properly in ages."

It took just one smell of the stew for Rowan to realise he was right. She dived in with gusto, and Mathew settled down beside her with his own bowl.

June and Willow woke up while they were eating, and after expressing their joy at Rowan's recovery, helped themselves to food too.

It was just starting to feel like things were back to normal when there came the rustling pound of footsteps outside and Alan crashed through the cave's entrance. He was sweat-soaked and out of breath. He barely had time to register surprise at Rowan's consciousness before the news poured out of him with the urgency of a rain-fed river.

"Marion's been arrested!"

The piece of bread Rowan had been raising to her mouth fell back into her bowl with a splash. Brown liquid splattered her shirt. She didn't notice.

"What?" she said, voice raspy with shock.

"I went into Nottingham," Alan said, leaning against the wall as he fought for breath. "To trade for supplies. An old friend of mine who works in the castle stables said Marion was brought in last night. The rumours say she was arrested for treason. The word on the street is that…" Alan paused, swallowed, bracing himself for the next words. "That they're going to execute her tomorrow."

Rowan surged to her feet. Her ribs screamed, her head span. She clenched her jaw and ignored both. She stumbled towards where her tunic lay by the fire. She reached instinctively for her bow and quiver, and then remembered with a jolt that they were still at the castle.

"Rowan!" said Mathew. "We can't go now. You're still hurt and so's June. We're in no shape to launch a rescue mission."

"We have to." Rowan tried to pull her tunic on

without jolting her ribs and failed. "Or at least, I do. It's only a rumour that the execution is tomorrow. It could be sooner. It could be right now."

Her fingers fumbled with panic as she yanked on her boots. Her mind filled with images of Marion alone in a dungeon, being led to the gallows, swinging from a rope…

"They won't kill her straight away," Mathew said. "They'll want to… question her first."

The word "question" settled over the cave like frost. Rowan felt her bruises throb. She remembered metal fists gleaming in the fire-dancing shadows. She remembered the stench of blood, snarling words curling around the point of a knife. *I will cut you away piece by piece…*

She flinched away from the memories. She imagined Marion's beautiful face breaking beneath mailed fists and her movements re-doubled. She finished with her boots and tried to stand upright. She had to lean against the wall, gasping for breath.

"Rowan," Willow said. "Slow down. Mathew's right. We all want to help Marion, but if we barge in as we are, we'll only get ourselves killed. We need a plan."

Rowan straightened up and stared at all of them. From the four fear-darkened faces that stared back at her, she could see that it was true, they did all want to help. But they were all tired. June's leg was still bandaged, and Rowan could hardly move. Willow was right. They needed some kind of strategy.

"OK," Rowan said, collapsing back to the cave floor and breathing deeply to try and calm her racing heart. "OK, let's make a plan. First things first, how do we get in?"

"That's not going to be easy," Alan said heavily.

"I can't see how we can get into the town, let alone the castle. They've got guards at the city gates checking everyone's faces. Everyone's heard Rowan's description now. They're not saying she's the Green Hood. They don't want to admit that a teenage girl's been robbing them all this time. They're just saying she's wanted for treason. Either way, Rowan can't go through the gates. The rest of us should be OK though." He paused and added darkly "For now."

The words hung like a stain on the air. Everyone knew what he meant. If Marion gave up their names and faces, it wasn't just them who were in danger but their families as well. If she had given up the location of their camp, there could be guards bearing down on them as they spoke.

Panic spiked higher in Rowan's chest. She fought to keep it down. *Don't think about it. Marion wouldn't do that. She would never betray you.*

"OK," Rowan said. It was now an effort to keep her voice calm. "So we can't use the gates. How else can we get in?"

"Over the walls?" said Mathew.

"Those walls were built to repel invaders," said Rowan. "Even if we could climb them, we'd be seen and shot before we reached the top."

"You did it," Alan pointed out. "The other day, that's how you got out of the town after the contest."

"That was just me alone. All of us together, no way we wouldn't be spotted, especially if there are more guards about."

Fire-crackled silence swallowed the words. It was June who broke it.

"There might be a way."

Every eye in the cave turned to her. Her face was pinched and scared, but determined.

"My aunt used to work in the castle," she went on. "In the kitchens. She told me that there are caves under the town that lead all the way out of it. They used to be escape routes if the castle was attacked, but now they're just used for storage. She told me where the entrance was beyond the town walls. I think... I think I can remember where it is."

More silence settled over them, sharp and glittering as shattered ice. Rowan looked at June, considering. It was well known that Nottingham was built on a honeycomb of sandstone caves. Some were small like the one they currently occupied, some vast and sprawling. If what June said was true, this could be their best way in. If she was remembering what her aunt told her correctly. If the entrance was where she thought it was. If the caves hadn't been blocked off. *If, if, if...*

"Even if we do get in, what then?" asked Willow. "There's just five of us, and two of us can barely walk. How are we meant to fight off a whole army?"

"We get an army of our own." The words were Mathew's, quiet and sure. They all turned to stare at him. His eyes were bright with the gleam of an idea, his cheeks flushed with excitement.

"June told us what Marion said," he said to Rowan. "About how the nobles fear the Green Hood because they're scared he, or rather you, will trigger an uprising. I say we give them what they fear. The people love you, Rowan. If you stood up and asked them to fight for you, they would."

"I couldn't ask anyone to do that. They'd be unarmed peasants up against trained soldiers. It would be a massacre!"

"There are more of us than there are of them," Mathew said. "This could be about more than rescuing Marion. She's the King's cousin, right? So what if we storm the castle, depose the Sheriff and put *her* in charge instead? She's of royal blood, so the nobles should accept her authority and she's known to be a sympathetic to the peasants plight, so they'll accept her too, hopefully."

"Mathew, what you're saying is impossible," Willow said, her eyes wide with wonder.

"It only seems impossible because nobody's ever tried it before," Mathew threw back. "Just imagine it. A Nottingham free of tyranny, where the nobles don't grow rich while the poor starve. It's what we've been working towards all these months. This is our chance to make that dream a reality. We have to take it."

Mathew looked around at them, his eyes ablaze with revolutionary fire, his hair crackling with the electricity of his words.

Rowan stared back at him, lost for words. What Mathew was suggesting was incredible, impossible, insane, and yet...

Rowan thought again of her parents, dead from the casual cruelty of the Sheriff's regime. She thought of all the people she had seen suffer and starve in Locksley and the other villages. She thought of Gisborne, hurling her against a wall as if she were nothing, a possession to be used and broken at his leisure. She wondered how many other girls he had done that to. She thought of Marion, with her soft lips and dark hair and whispered words. Marion, who had saved her life and was now facing death as a result. Marion, who was everything to her and more.

She realised that it didn't matter how impossible

the odds were. She would do whatever it took to get Marion back.

"Alright," she said, her voice low and gravelly with determination. "Let's do it. Let's make the bastards pay."

"Wait." Junes voice dropped into the cave like a stone. They all looked at her. Her broad face was solemn, her brow heavy.

"You know I've nothing against Marion," she said, speaking more carefully than Rowan had ever heard her before. "Not anymore. But let's face it, how is putting another noble in charge going to help us in the long run?"

Rowan felt flames curl around her stomach. "She's not just 'another noble'," she snapped, temper shortened by pain. "She's Marion. We know her!"

"We know her now," June ploughed on. "But once she gets a taste of real power…"

She spread her hands, letting the sentence trail.

"She's not like that!" Rowan was halfway to her feet again, her fists clenched at her sides. For the first time, she was thinking back to that fight with June all those months ago. The urge for a rematch was burning bright within her, injuries be damned.

"It doesn't matter if she is or isn't." Now it was Willow who spoke up. Her voice was calm, her eyes steady as they found Rowan's.

"Like it or not, Marion's not going to live forever. We don't know who will come after her. As long as the present system's in place, there will always be the risk of oppression."

Rowan sat back, breathing deeply to calm the roaring in her blood. Much as she wanted to scream them all down, she knew that they were right. She loved Marion to the depths of her soul, knew that she would lead Nottingham well and fairly, that she would care for the people and never let that power corrupt her. But she also knew that as long as the nobles were ranked above the peasants, there would be no peace for the latter. By putting Marion in charge, they'd just be propping up that same twisted system.

Now Mathew spoke up. "You're right," he said, nodding to Willow and June. "But we can't deal with that right now. If we rise up tomorrow and don't put someone in charge that the other lords would recognise as a leader, they'll just take over themselves, put one of their own in charge, maybe someone even worse. Marion's the only noble currently on our side. Let's use that, for the short term at least, worry about dismantling the system later."

Alan nodded, planting himself firmly on Mathew's side as usual. Willow and June looked at each other, having a conversation no one else could hear. Rowan watched them, pulse racing. Every second they spent debating this was time they weren't preparing; time the Sheriff's men could be hurting the girl she loved.

At last, June looked up, her brow heavy but her face open. "Ok," she said. "Just as long as we all agree that this is a temporary fix, yes?"

Everyone nodded. Rowan felt the tightness inside her ease a little.

"Right then," she said, getting to her feet more slowly this time. "Let's assume the rumours about Marion's execution are true. That gives us till dawn to prepare."

She looked out at the sky beyond the cave's entrance. The sun was already past its highest point. It would be dark soon. Marion's last night on earth, if they weren't successful.

"If this is to work, we need to be ready," she went on. "That means we need every bow to be oiled and supple, every blade sharp, as many arrows fletched as we can."

The others nodded. Rowan met each of their gazes. Their faces were pale and scared, but they met her eyes with a fierce determination that stirred her heart. She realised that if it came to it, there was no one else in whose company she would rather die in.

"Let's get to work. We leave before first light."

CHAPTER TWENTY-ONE

They had not locked Marion in the castle dungeon as she might have feared, but in what was clearly one of the guest rooms. It was small and sparsely furnished, but when Marion compared it to how Rowan had been treated, beaten to a pulp in that tiny tower room, her blood boiled at the injustice.

For the rest of that night and the following day, she had sat and stewed and paced. The guards who brought her food responded to her questions and demands with stony silence. Now, as evening painted the sky beyond the small window in shades of pink and gold, she heard a rattle of a key in the lock.

She turned to face it as the door swung open. She was surprised to see the Sheriff himself step in. She had been expecting another guardsman, here to beat answers out of her as they had for Rowan. She didn't know whether to be relieved or more scared as the man surveyed her with his cold eyes. A smug smile twisted the edge of his mouth, like a hunter surveying a fat rabbit in a trap.

No, she told herself firmly. *Don't be a rabbit. Be a wolf or a lion or a hawk. Be fierce and brave. Be like Rowan.*

She straightened her spine, forced her face into a look of haughty disdain.

"Apologies for keeping you waiting so long, my lady," the Sheriff said. "As you know, a fugitive escaped this castle two days ago, and I've been busy trying to find the culprit."

"I do not see what that has to do with me," Marion said, adopting an imperious tone to hide the quiver in her voice.

The Sheriff spread his hands. "Murder has been committed, my lady," he said silkily. "I'm afraid that no one is above suspicion.

"Murder?"

"Of Sir Guy." The Sheriff eyed her with cool appraisal as he spoke. "Killed in the fugitive's room."

Gisborne was dead. The words hit her like a slap. She hadn't thought Rowan capable of such things. But when she thought of the girl she loved lying bruised and broken in that cave, Marion found that she was not sorry. Gisborne was a vile man who deserved all he got. If his death had ensured Rowan's escape, then it was worth it.

"Surely you cannot be suggesting that I had anything to do with that," Marion said, hoping that she sounded outraged rather than scared.

The Sheriff stared at her; his pale face smooth as marble. "You were the last person seen to enter the fugitive's cell before Gisborne himself. That makes you one of the last people to see him alive."

He tilted his head, his smile vicious and cutting as a blade. "I'm curious, did you and the outlaw girl kill him together or did you simply leave her a weapon and let her do your dirty work?" The Sheriff paused, savouring Marion's panicked silence. "Your father used to be Lord of Locksley, precisely where this girl was from. Did you meet her then? Decide to use her now to eliminate the man who took your father's lands?"

Oh, he was clever. Far cleverer than she had ever realised. She had hoped that as she was a woman, he would dismiss her as a threat. But unlike Gisborne, the Sheriff did not make the mistake of underestimating his victims.

"This is ridiculous," Marion said. Her rabbit heart was pounding faster, as if she were running, fleeing from this man as she so longed to do. "You have no proof."

"I'm afraid that we do," the Sheriff said carelessly. "Your father proved most helpful with a little... persuasion."

Dread dropped into Marion's stomach. Her father couldn't know anything of importance. Could he?

"He said that you left the evening of Gisborne's death and did not return until much later," the Sheriff went on. "He said you also left the following morning and that he hadn't seen you since. Your servants confirmed the story."

The Sheriff's flat eyes met hers. "Where were you, Lady Marion?"

"I... I..." Marion scrambled to come up with a lie he would believe. "I went riding."

"Odd time to go for a ride. Did anyone see you go?"

"I... I went alone," Marion said. "I prefer it that way."

"I see."

Marion's heart was thrumming river-fast now. She could feel the jaws of the trap closing around her. She opted for outrage once more, trying to hide her fear.

"If my father is here, I demand to see him."

"Regrettably, that won't be possible." The Sheriff examined his fingernails with a bored air. "I'm afraid that shortly after we questioned him, he passed away."

The words hit her like a plunge into icy water. She was falling, drowning, her mind full of blank white shock.

"You… You killed him." The words were a gasp, dragged from cold-ravaged lungs.

The Sheriff smiled, a hard, sharp thing, all ice and venom. "He was an old man, my lady. Many things kill old men. Stress, exhaustion, the shock of knowing his only daughter could commit such heinous acts…"

"Stop it!" She could feel a wave of grief surging within her, but she held it back with all her will, forcing herself to think clearly.

She realised that whatever protection she'd had was also dead. She may still be the King's cousin, but that meant far less when that King was far away fighting a foreign war and his brother did not regard Marion with the same favour.

By the way the Sheriff was looking at her, Marion thought he must be thinking the same thing. The points of his teeth glinted as he smiled.

"I promised the people a hanging," he said. "I'd hate to disappoint them. But it need not be your neck on the line. Help me find the perpetrator of this vile crime, and I will forgive your part in it."

Marion swallowed. Her throat was suddenly very dry. "What makes you think I know anything about it?"

"Let's not play this game any longer," the Sheriff said, a bite of annoyance hardening his words. "We both know that you helped the Fletcher girl escape. Perhaps you even know where she and the other outlaws are hiding. Tell me where they are and not only will I spare your life, I will grant you back your father's lands. I will give you more power and influence than any woman in your position could expect. It is a good offer, my lady, I suggest that you consider it quite closely."

Marion stared into those dead eyes. She thought of the little cave in the forest, so cosy and vulnerable. She imagined watching Rowan, Mathew and the others hanging from the scaffold in the castle courtyard, people who had been kind to her, who had accepted her for who she was. She thought of returning to Locksley Manor, of living there alone for the rest of her days. It was no choice at all.

"I am sorry, my lord Sheriff," she said, keeping her voice as calm and even as she could. "I cannot help you."

The Sheriff appraised her. Not a flicker of emotion crossed his face, but she felt a blast of icy rage. Her spirit shivered, but she forced herself to stand tall, to meet the predator's gaze.

"Very well," the Sheriff said at last. "I'll give you the night to think it over. But in the morning, I shall ask you again, and then I shall not be so lenient."

With that, he turned away. Marion heard the door locking behind him, leaving her alone with the gathering shadows.

❈ ❈ ❈

Rowan drew back her bow and her ribs shrieked. She let it go slack and doubled over, gasping.

The sun was sinking low in the sky, glaring at her

as red as a demon's eye. After a frenzied afternoon of arrow fletching, knife sharpening and going over the plan again and again, Rowan had left the others preparing an evening meal and headed out into the woods to practise her bow work ahead of tomorrow.

It wasn't proving easy. Every little movement set her bones on fire. How could she rescue Marion if she couldn't even draw a bow? How was she good for anything without that?

Gritting her teeth, she straightened and pulled back again, trying to fix on the target. Her vision blurred and swam. Her head pounded. Her arms shook with the strain. Her mind blazed red, red, red…

Mailed fists broke her apart over and over… hard hands pinned her against a wall… *Make me happy for a few minutes… She's no one, a nothing…* The point of a dagger wept red against her cheek… *I will cut you away piece by piece…*

She felt the sickening slip of a blade into flesh, heard Gisborne's last gurgling breaths, felt the warm mist on her skin as the knife pulled free.

She let her bow drop to her side. She slumped against a tree, breathing heavily, one hand clutching her ribs. She took her pounding head in her hands, rubbing her thumbs into her eyes as if she could wipe away the memories.

She thought of Marion, alone in the castle, just as she had been. She thought of a knife pushed into bound hands, *I love you* breathed against bloody lips.

The steel inside her hardened to stone. She would not let them take Marion from her. Not now, not ever.

She straightened, staring down at her bow. She wished she still had the one her father had made for her, but it was back at the castle, maybe lost forever. She was borrowing June's, who had always preferred her axe anyway. The bow felt stiff and unfamiliar, as if it knew she wasn't its true owner. Still, it was a good bow, and she needed to get used to it if she was to have any hope of rescuing Marion.

"The trick is not to think too much," her father's voice whispered in her mind. She remembered his big gentle hands positioning her small ones on her first bow. "You spend too long fixating on the target and your arm tenses up and it spoils your aim. Better just to trust your instincts. Don't think. Just look, draw and loose."

Rowan looked up at the target, pinning it with her eyes. In one swift movement, she raised her bow, drew it back and let it loose.

The arrow struck the centre of the target she had drawn on a tree more than a hundred paces away. Rowan allowed herself a small smile. She was ready.

CHAPTER TWENTY-TWO

Rowan and the others skirted the edge of the town's wall, keeping low, senses primed for the sound of attack. If they were spotted before they even reached the caves, this would all be for nothing.

Willow had given Rowan a mixture of herbs to help the pain. She had chewed on it, gagging on the bitterness. It had helped somewhat, dulling the sharpness in her ribs to a rumbling ache, but they still twinged with every step. She ignored it and kept going. The sun was already creeping into the sky. Marion didn't have long left.

Finally, they came to an iron grating in the grass. June heaved it open, and a smell of old stone and cobwebs belched up from within. Peering down, Rowan could see rough stone steps descending into darkness. She swallowed. This was it.

Alan pulled a pitch-dipped torch from his belt and lit it with his strike fire. Then one by one they creeped down the steps into the dust-scented dark.

The caves were as black and twisted as guts. There were so many turns and sudden dead-ends that it was impossible to tell where they were actually going.

It occurred to Rowan that they might be actually heading *away* from the castle, away from Marion. She could already be swinging above them while they wandered this endless tangle of tunnels. Rowan fought to unhook the claws of anxiety and forced herself to keep going.

In the flickering half-light of the torch, she could make out the tunnel walls, smooth and pale yellow, marked in places by the scars left by chisels. Her father taught her that some of these caves had formed naturally and others had been carved out by hand from the soft sandstone, to make cellars, homes and businesses. Many of them had then been joined together to form this sprawling network of passages.

The floor underfoot was sandy and uneven. The torch cast dancing shadows which stretched to grotesque shapes as they passed. Time moved strangely in this barely-lit, subterranean world. It felt like they had been walking for hours, though it could have been mere minutes when they at last came to a wide rounded cave stacked with barrels. More rough-cut steps led up one wall to a wooden trapdoor in the ceiling.

Her insides swooping with hope, Rowan took the torch from Alan and darted forwards, scrambling up the steps. She lifted the trapdoor a finger's width and peered out.

She was hit at once with a blast of voices and the smell of spilt ale. A wooden bar partly obscured her view, and beyond it she could make out a dim, cramped space. There were benches and tables lined with people drinking, talking and laughing. Lead sunk into her stomach.

"It's a tavern," she whispered down to the others. "We're in its cellar. We must have taken a wrong turn further back."

Muffled groans from the dark behind her. Still, at least this meant that they were within the city walls if not the castle ones. It might take them hours to find another way out, so they decided to take this one.

Rowan waited until the barmaid was distracted clearing a table then ushered the others up one by one. They mingled with the tavern's clientele, slipping out into the bright morning beyond when no one was watching.

Rowan led the others into the shadows down the side of the pub, out of reach of the guard's prying eyes. They were on the edge of the town square. Before them, the castle gates rose up like a frown against the sky. The gallows stood on a raised dais in the square's centre. People were already beginning to gather around it.

Nervous anticipation thrummed in the air. Word had gotten out that a noblewoman was to be hung that morning. Execution of nobles was rare, and the excitement was palpable. Rowan was sickened by it.

She eyed the castle gates. The portcullis was lowered and flanked with guards. Still more patrolled the ramparts above or wandered the crowd in the square, fingering their swords, armour gleaming in the morning sun.

Rowan shrank further into the shadows. Her eyes scanned the castle for a way in while behind her the others debated the best way for her to get her message to the crowd. She would need to move to somewhere clear and open, which would leave her open to attack. Rowan's eyes fell on the gallows on its raised platform, the tallest point around, right at the centre of the square. She knew what she must do.

Before any of the others could think to stop her, she ran out into the square, leapt onto the platform, grabbed the rope of the noose and heaved herself up to the top of the scaffold. She stood, wobbling slightly, trying to silence the pain pounding at her skull. The beam was barely thicker than her boots, but she told herself it was no different from balancing on a branch in the forest.

She heard gasps of surprise from the assembled crowd, voices exclaiming in wonder.

"It's the Green Hood!"

Faces tuned in her direction, pinning her with their stares. After so long spent hiding, her stomach squirmed at the attention, her skin prickling beneath the weight of so many eyes. But it didn't matter; this had to be done.

"People of Nottingham," she called, and this time she made no attempt to disguise her voice but let it ring out clear and true. "You have been wronged. You have been oppressed and deceived by those who call themselves your masters. The money you need to survive has been taken from you, just to make the rich even richer, while your children starve. It is time we rid ourselves of this *parasite* who calls himself Sheriff."

An arrow whizzed past, so close that it tore the sleeve of her tunic and scratched the skin beneath. Rowan looked up at the battlements in time to see a second arrow fly back in reply, taking the man responsible in the throat.

The other outlaws ran forward and spread out to surround the platform, training their loaded bows on the men at the battlements or guards in the crowd. No more arrows came.

Rowan turned back to the crowd, trying to hide

how much her legs were shaking. She couldn't falter now, couldn't flinch.

"You've called me a legend," she said, swallowing the dryness from her throat. "A myth."

She pulled the scarf down from her face.

"But as you can see, I am neither."

She dropped the leather mask to the ground.

"I am one of you."

She pushed back her hood, exposing her bruised face. The morning sun transformed her hair to woven bronze. Gasps and cries of shock rippled through the crowd.

"Like you, I have known suffering and hunger," Rowan shouted above the noise. "I watched my father hang from a gallows just like this one for the crime of feeding his family. How many of you have lost friends and loved ones in the same way?"

From the corner of her eye, Rowan saw Roderick emerge from the alley to his forge. He leaned on his hammer as he gazed up at her. There was a look in his eyes as strengthening as hot mead. It gave her the courage she needed to carry on.

"I ask you now to stand with me. We must cast down the men who crush us, so we can truly have freedom. Will you fight with me?"

Silence. No sound but the pounding of blood in her ears. It was over. It hadn't worked. Marion would die, and there was nothing she could do.

She caught a flash of movement at the edge of her vision. One of the guards had crept closer while she had been talking, and now he had a drawn and loaded bow trained on her. He was too close to miss, and there was no time to even duck. His fingers loosened on the string...

Then Roderick was there, smashing his hammer into the bow and then the man's ribs. The guard folded like windblown grass, crumbling to the ground in a groaning heap.

"Listen!" Roderick roared, his strong voice carrying much further than Rowan's had managed. "This girl has fed your families, defended your lives. She has bled for you and fought for you and risked her life for you. Will you turn your backs now when she needs your help? Together we are strong. Together we can fight them and we can win!"

He raised his hammer high. "For the Green Hood!"

All over the square, the cry was taken up. It swelled until it roared like a dragon, like a thunderstorm, like an angry sea.

Weapons were seized, people grabbing whatever came to hand. Spades, pitchforks, meat hooks, kitchen knives, branding irons. The guards were overwhelmed, their swords taken. People poured into Roderick's forge, stripping it of the weapons he had been forced to make for the castle guards.

Rowan saw a guardsman make it to the platform, climbing up towards her with bow in hand. Before he could so much as nock an arrow, she had leapt from the gallows, using the rope to swing around and boot him in the chest, throwing him off the platform and into the teeth of the mob.

In a second, June was beside her, tearing away her scarf and hefting her axe in readiness. Side by side they fought, Rowan shooting down approaching guards and June swinging her axe into any that were able to get close enough. Around them, Willow, Alan and Mathew loosed arrows into all the guards they could see.

The crowd was surging forwards. A roar was building. "To the gates! To the gates!"

June and Rowan jumped down from the platform and let the tide of people carry them to the castle gates. The portcullis was still down, the men who had been guarding it long since fled. Through the thick grating, Rowan could make out the wheel that would lift it, frustratingly out of reach.

Arrows were raining down on them from above. Already people were falling. This would turn into a bloodbath if they couldn't get the gate open right now.

Rowan turned to June. "Can you lift it?"

June's eyes widened. She stared at the heavy, blackened oak of the portcullis. She nodded.

"Only for a moment."

"A moment is all we need."

June hunkered down before the portcullis, taking a beam in each of her large hands. Rowan barked at Mathew, Willow and Alan to defend them, then crouched beside her. They shared a nod.

June gave a tremendous heave, her face reddening with the effort. Slowly, the iron-plated spikes at the base of the portcullis rose above the ground. Rowan slipped through the narrow gap just as June's strength failed her and the spikes smashed back into the mud where Rowan had been only a second before.

Rowan came up in a crouch, grinning at June in amazement.

June was on her knees, breathing heavily. She looked up, and her eyes widened. "Behind you!"

Rowan twisted around, just in time to see the guard running for her, sword raised. In an eye blink, she had an arrow drawn, nocked and loosed. It hit the man at point-blank range, going clean through his eye and sprouting from the back of his skull. He fell without a sound, revealing another man behind him.

Rowan ducked his first sword swing, spun away on her knees, came fully upright with Marion's knife in one hand. She ripped it across his throat in a spray of scarlet. He fell away with a splutter.

Rowan lunged for the winch, pulling it around with all the strength she had. Slowly, the portcullis rose, helped by many hands beneath it. The crowd poured forth, filling the courtyard like a river from a broken dam, rushing for the keep.

Arrows continued to rain down on them from all sides, but already people were running up the steps along the walls to deal with the archers.

The crowd reached the great oak doors, beating on them with a hundred fists. But they were barred from the inside and didn't shift. June tried to shoulder barge the doors, but she just bounced off the heavy oak as if she were a fly.

"Find a battering ram," Rowan roared over the thunder of the crowd. "Something to break down the doors, hurry!"

A group of fighters peeled away from the main throng and ran for the stables. They attacked one of the wooden beams holding up the roof, battering at it with clubs and hammers until it shuddered free.

Even with it, Rowan knew they were unlikely to get inside in time to save Marion. Her eyes fell on a coil of rope hanging up in the stables. She dashed to fetch it, piercing one end with an arrow and threading it onto the shaft as she ran back to the wall.

"Are you mad?" June cried when she saw what

Rowan planned to do. "You said climbing the walls wouldn't work."

"I said it wouldn't be subtle," Rowan replied, nocking the arrow to her bow and eyeing the lowest window, some twenty feet above. "I think they've noticed we're here."

She drew back her bow and let the arrow fly. It thudded into the wood of the window ledge. She gave the rope a hearty tug. It felt like it should hold.

She slipped her bow across her back and turned to the other four outlaws gathered around her with nervous expressions. But none of them dared suggest she didn't try, and for that she was grateful.

"You're in charge until I get back," Rowan told June. The big girl nodded solemnly.

Rowan turned to the other three. "Cover me as best you can."

She looked into each of their faces, wanting to say more. She couldn't face saying goodbye, couldn't bear the thought that she might never see them again.

Without another word, June ran off to help with the battering ram, and the other three took up their positions to defend Rowan's ascent. Rowan turned back to the rope and began the climb.

Her ribs burned savagely with every heave upwards. Her boots scrambled for purchase on the uneven stone of the castle wall. Her muscles screamed in protest, her hands tearing on the rough rope.

Arrows flew around her, and she was acutely aware that it would take just one hit, one arrow in her arm or shoulder to send her tumbling to the courtyard below. She could feel the rhythmic pounding of the battering ram on the door shivering up through the wall, as if the castle was trying to shake her off.

She battled on, thinking of Marion and nothing else. Marion scared. Marion alone. Marion dying if she didn't keep going, if she didn't keep putting one hand over the other.

As she neared the top, she felt the rope give a little. Looking up, she saw that her weight was slowly pulling the arrow free of the wood. She lunged for the window frame just as the arrow came completely loose, clattering to the courtyard below.

Rowan was left dangling from the windowsill, her ribs shrieking, her sweaty hands clawing the splintered wood. Grasping, choking, praying, she gave a tremendous heave and dragged herself up and over the windowsill, rolling safely into the cool stone corridor beyond.

For a moment she just lay there below the window, breathing deeply and marvelling at the fact she was still alive. Then there came the ring of footsteps behind her, coming rapidly up the corridor.

Shaking, her limbs wobbly as a newborn fawn's, she got to her feet and hurried away down the passage. She hid behind a tapestry as a patrol of guards went rushing past her, heading down to the entrance hall.

She remained hidden after they had gone, waiting for her heartbeat to return to normal. She tried not to focus on how vulnerable she was. No sword, no armour, only an unfamiliar bow, a handful of arrows and Marion's little knife. It would have to do.

Drawing her bow and a single arrow, she stepped from her hiding place and set off into the belly of the castle.

CHAPTER TWENTY-THREE

The Sheriff was dressing in his chambers when it started. The roaring of an angry sea, then a great, rhythmic crashing. He dismissed his servants and headed out into the corridors to locate the trouble.

The banging, pounding and shouting only grew louder as he moved through the castle. He met the captain of the guards coming the other way up the corridor. The man was sweaty and breathless, his eyes darting like a cornered animal.

"What the hell is going on?" the Sheriff said.

"The people have risen up, my lord."

"Risen up? What is this nonsense?"

"They've armed themselves. They've breached the front gates. I believe they intend to take the castle. We're holding them in the courtyard for now, but I don't know for how long. I'm sending all my remaining men to the entrance hall to hold them off."

The man lowered his eyes, suddenly unable to meet his master's gaze. "They are led by the Green Hood."

The Sheriff fought the urge to take the captain's head in his hands and crush his skull like an egg. He stamped down the fury, moulding it into something cold, calm, controlled. Something he could use.

The Green Hood. Well, if that wretched girl was back here, it could only be for one reason.

"Have Lady Marion brought to my chambers," the Sheriff said, already turning to stride back the way he had come. It was time to rid himself of this menace once and for all.

✣ ✣ ✣

Rowan moved through the castle as cautiously as she would the forest at night. She slipped into doorways or around corners to avoid the running guards and panicking servants.

She didn't know if she should be heading down to the dungeons or if the Sheriff would keep Marion hidden away in one of the towers. It would take hours to check the whole castle, in which time she would definitely be caught and killed. Besides, she didn't even know how to get to the dungeons. She hadn't exactly had a guided tour of the castle on her last visit, and they hadn't been so thoughtful as to put up signs.

Then, just as she was stiffening with indecision, she rounded a bend in the corridor and saw an open door before her. Within, the Sheriff stood grinning at her. Held against him, with a knife to her throat, was Marion.

Rowan didn't think, didn't pause for breath or consideration. She nocked the arrow and drew it back as she rushed forwards, her bow aimed at what little of the Sheriff's face she could see.

"Let her go!" shouted Rowan.

At the same time, Marion cried out, "No Rowan, run!"

The door slammed closed behind her. Glancing over her shoulder, she saw two armoured men stepping out from either side of the doorway, swords levelled at Rowan's back.

"I think not," said the Sheriff. His eyes were bright with triumph, his grin sharp enough to cut skin. "I knew you'd come for her, just as she came for you. I don't know what unnatural *friendship* has passed between you, but unless you want to watch her die, you will put down your weapon and surrender."

Rowan heard the guards step closer, felt the points of their swords prick her spine. She cursed herself for being so foolish.

She looked away from the Sheriff's face and into Marion's. Her dark eyes were sharp with defiance. Silently, they begged Rowan not to give in. Rowan hoped her own eyes said that she didn't plan on it. Her mind was racing.

Slowly, she let her bowstring go slack.

"Trust you to think love is unnatural," she said, crouching down to lower the weapon to the floor.

The Sheriff gave a mirthless bark of laughter. "Love won't save you now. Believe me, by the time we're finished, you'll wish that I'd let Gisborne have —"

With the bow almost at the floor, Rowan pulled back the bowstring and loosed the arrow. It shuddered into the Sheriff's thigh. He bellowed like a stuck boar.

Marion took advantage of his distraction, wrenching the knife away from her neck and crunching an elbow into his face. The Sheriff staggered away from her, doubled over, clutching at his nose and leg.

Rowan, still crouched low, slammed her bow into the legs of the nearest guard, knocking him off his feet. She brought a knee up into his face as he fell.

She sprang up and spun to meet the next man, dodging the first swipe of his sword. But she wasn't quick enough to avoid the follow-up punch to her jaw. Stunned and staggering, there was nothing she could do to stop him from throwing her against the wall. She felt her skull grate against cold stone.

He swung his sword for her neck. She just got her bow up in time so the blade bit into wood not flesh, almost severing the weapon in half.

The guard drew back his sword for another blow, but before he could land it, Marion was there, smashing a stool over his head. He went down.

Marion grabbed Rowan's hand. "Come on, we've got to go…"

But the Sheriff was upright once more, limping over to block the door. His sword was drawn, his eyes boiling.

"You're not going anywhere," he spat. Blood spurted from his broken nose, staining his beard auburn. "If you're so keen to be together, you can die together."

Rowan cast the broken bow aside and snatched up the sword of one of the fallen guards. Marion hefted a broken stool leg like a club.

Below them came a colossal crash, then a triumphant roar. Rowan felt her heart leap.

"It's over, d'Aubigny," she said. "The people have taken the castle. You're finished."

The Sheriff's face was a bloodied snarl. "Not while I still stand. While I deal with you, my men will slaughter your rabble. Then your head will hang from the ramparts to show what happens to traitors."

He lunged for them. Rowan forced herself between him and Marion, rushing to block his thrust. Rowan may have known how to fight, but she was still just a teenager, injured and exhausted, who had only ever practised swordplay with her father using wooden staffs. He was a nobleman twice her age, who had been trained in swordplay since he could walk. It was all she could do to hold off his barrage of blows, let alone land her own. Her arms ached with every swing. Her bones shook with every parry.

The Sheriff waited for a gap in her guard, then crunched his fist into her injured ribs. Rowan stumbled backwards, bent double and choking. Before the Sheriff could press his advantage, Marion was on him, catching him across the face with her stool-leg club.

The Sheriff staggered, but maintained his footing, swiping for Marion instead. She managed to block the blow with the club, the blade sinking into the wood. With a twist of his wrist, the Sheriff sent the club spinning from her grip.

Unarmed, Marion backed away, forced into a corner as the Sheriff advanced. Rowan straightened, shaking off the pain and threw herself at him, swinging her sword for his head.

The Sheriff turned just in time to parry the blow. His blade dropped, striking for her guts. Rowan twisted at the last second, and the blade skimmed across her side instead.

Rowan cried out, staggered, her mind frozen with shock. She felt blood soaking through her tunic, hot and red as winter wine.

The Sheriff slammed the pommel of his sword into

her chin, knocking her to the floor. He kicked the sword from her grip and stamped down on her chest, holding her in place. He rested the sword tip against her breast bone, just above her frantic heart.

"No!" Marion screamed as she flew at him, all fists and teeth. The Sheriff struck her across the face. She crumpled to her knees. The Sheriff seized her by the hair, wrenching her head up to look at Rowan.

"Watch," he said calmly. "Let me show you just how worthless your *beloved* Green Hood really is."

He placed his foot over Rowan's wound, slowly pressing down until the girl screamed and writhed.

Marion struggled, tried to break free, but his fingers were like iron hooks in her hair and they held her still.

"You see!" The Sheriff's face was a mask of blood and twisted joy. "She's not a legend or a hero. She's nothing but vermin, a rabid bitch in need of putting down."

Slowly, he raised the sword.

Marion's face was pale and tight, her eyes swimming with tears.

Rowan held the other girl's gaze with her own, trying to tell her without words to be brave, that it was going to be alright. The knife Marion had given her was hidden in her curled fist.

As the sword hovered in the air, Rowan shot up, sinking the blade into the inside of the Sheriff's thigh and twisting it sharply. The Sheriff's roar shook the castle.

Rowan wrenched the knife free. The Sheriff lurched and groaned. He let go of Marion and sank to one knee, his face chalk white, fingers clutching for the life pouring down his leg.

In a heartbeat, Marion grabbed Rowan's fallen

sword and thrust it into the Sheriff's chest, until the cross guard jolted against his ribs.

The Sheriff's drained face turned to her, his features stretched wide and gulping, unable to believe what they had done to him. He slumped to the ground like a falling tree, his cold eyes unmoving and lifeless.

Far away, the battle boomed and crashed, the sounds distant and unreal. Rowan tried to get up and almost passed out. Hot, molten agony was pouring through her side, slipping through her fingers in slick, red gusts.

She felt soft hands on her face, warm arms around her. She looked up into a pair of eyes, dark as moonless nights and dreamless sleep. She felt the feather-touch of raven curls against her skin.

"Marion…" The name brushed her lips like a sigh, like a prayer.

"Sshhh," Marion whispered. "Don't try to talk. Help will come along soon, I promise. Just lie still."

"Marion," Rowan breathed again. It felt so good to say it, so good to see her again. A weak smile creased the corners of her eyes.

❈ ❈ ❈

When Willow and June made it into the castle, they found Marion and Rowan in that same room, with three bodies. Marion had Rowan's head cradled in her lap, pressing a hand to her side and murmuring soft reassurances.

Willow ran to them at once, crouching to examine Rowan's wound while June paced the room between the dead Sheriff and unconscious guards.

"It's not as bad as it looks," Rowan said between clenched teeth. Her face was grey and slicked with sweat. Blood was soaking through her tunic.

Willow peeled back the layers to examine the wound. It gaped like a toothless mouth, vomiting red. But it was a straight, clean slash and not particularly deep. Rowan was right, it could have been a lot worse. Still...

"The Sheriff had a personal physician here in the castle," Marion said as Alan barrelled into the room.

Willow nodded, straightened and grabbed her brother by the collar.

"Find him and bring him here, at sword point if you have to."

She shoved him away and Alan took off down the corridor, throwing perplexed glances over his shoulder. June barrelled after him to help. Willow ripped the scarf from her own throat and pressed it to the wound, ignoring Rowan's groans of protest.

Mathew approached. His face was gleaming with sweat and he was bleeding from a cut above his eye, but he didn't seem to care. His eyes were bright, wide and shining.

"We did it, Rowan," he said, his voice hushed and breathless. "We've taken the castle. The guards that are still alive have been imprisoned, and the lords loyal to the Sheriff have surrendered. We've won!"

CHAPTER TWENTY-FOUR

Rowan sat on the battlements at the highest point of the castle. Beyond the muddy sprawl of the town, past the spread of harvested fields, she could make out the shaggy line of the forest. Fiery colours were eating up the green of the trees. Summer was finally over. But she had a feeling that this winter wouldn't be as bleak as the last one.

The wound in her side gave a twinge as she shifted her position. It still hurt, but she knew it was healing. Her ribs ached too, but it was a dim, distant kind of hurt, easily ignored. Every day she felt herself getting a little stronger. Soon she'd be flying through the trees as fast as an arrow again.

The Sheriff's physician had been found and, under the stern gaze of four drawn blades, had grudgingly cleaned and stitched up Rowan's cut.

"It is just a flesh wound," he said rather tetchily once he had finished. "Even so, she shouldn't be doing anything too exacting for some time." *Like starting revolutions* his scowling gaze said.

Rowan heard the soft sound of footsteps behind her. She looked over her shoulder to see Marion approaching. She had her hands clasped before her; fingers tangled in her skirts.

Rowan swivelled around, gripping the rough stone wall with both hands. Heights had never bothered her, but Marion always had the power to make her dizzy.

"My lady Sheriff," Rowan said with the hint of a smirk, bowing her head respectfully.

Marion's nervous expression became a scowl that instantly broke into laughter. "You don't have to call me that," she said, grinning. "Not ever, you understand?"

"Ah, but it suits you so well.,"

"I won't be Sheriff for long anyway."

Rowan laughed. "Did June get to you?"

"Well, she's right. We can do more. My family name doesn't make me a better ruler than you or June or Mathew—"

"I know," Rowan said, gently, "but that's a fight for another day. We all need to rest now."

There was a long silence. Marion twisted her hands together, seemed unable to meet Rowan's eyes.

"I never said... after the battle and everything..." she began, her voice stilted and unsure. "What you did, starting the uprising, risking your life, getting hurt... I can't thank you enough."

"It's alright," Rowan said at once. "It was all Mathew's idea really." The attempt at lightness struck her as false, and she inwardly cursed herself for speaking at all. "Anyway, you saved me," she added hastily, "when I was imprisoned, so it's only fair."

Rowan swallowed. Her throat constricted; her chest tightened as if she were drowning. She took a deep breath. There was something else she needed to say, that she had been meaning to say for some time.

"That time in the tower, before you left, you said something to me and I didn't say it back and…"

"That's OK," said Marion. "You didn't have to say anything, that's not why I said it."

"I know. But even so, I should have said it because it would have been true. That is, I mean, it is true…"

Rowan stammered into silence. She stared down at her boots, her face burning. Neither of them spoke for several moments. Rowan considered throwing herself off the battlements just to get away from the awkwardness. But she couldn't have moved if she'd wanted to. She seemed to be sealed to the wall she sat upon. She felt as fragile as an early leaf, waiting for winter's frost to snuff her out.

It was Marion who broke the silence. "You know, the people down there still call you the Green Hood."

Rowan looked up. Marion was staring past her into the town below. "I think some of them even believe that you're some great strapping man."

Rowan shrugged. "It doesn't matter. The Green Hood's not me, not really."

Marion smiled at her, raising a wry eyebrow. "Oh? And who are you *really*?"

Rowan stood up. She felt scared and bold all at once.

"I'm Rowan Fletcher."

She took a step towards Marion.

"I'm no longer an outlaw."

Another step.

"And I'm yours."

She was standing very close to Marion now, so close their noses were almost touching. So close they shared each other's breath.

Rowan lost herself in the starry depths of Marion's eyes. She breathed in her sweet scent. Blood thundered in her ears.

Marion's words were a sigh. They brushed Rowan's lips, soft as thistledown.

"And I'm yours."

Rowan took Marion's face in both hands. They kissed. It was so similar and so different from their last kiss in that tiny room which stank of blood and pain. It tasted of high, cold air and wild possibility. It tasted fresh and fizzing and bursting with promise. It tasted of something new, beginning at last.

ACKNOWLEDGEMENTS

First of all, I'd like to thank Gem, for picking out this book and believing in it, and for your patience, kindness and understanding. I'm sorry that things didn't quite go how we planned, but please know how much better you made this book with your insight, creativity and keen editor's eye.

To Harry, thank you for giving up your time and energy to talk to me about albinism, helping me create Mathew and making him the best version of himself. I love him and I promise to never make anything bad happen to him. (Don't trust writers, we make stuff up for a living.)

My wonderful sister Amy, thank you so so much for being my loudest cheerleader and the best soundboard for my ideas. Thank you for your endless enthusiasm and encouragement. Thank you for late night talks, shared jokes, countless games of Guess What Song is Stuck in my Head and everything else you do.

Thank you, Ellie, for the gorgeous front cover, it is a literal work of art. Thank you for your kind words, honest feedback and hours of hard work.

Thank you, Josh, for designing the website, helping me with all the scary techno-wizardry and for providing a "youthful perspective" on my young adult book.

Thank you to my parents, for fostering in me a love of both books and the outdoors, for giving me a safe place to live while I wrote this and for telling literally everyone in the county about it.

Thank you to everyone who proofread, offered feedback or listened to me blather about this book, including but not limited to Alex, Tim, Jo, Hannah, and I'm sure many others who I can't remember, for which I apologise, but know that you are here too.

Thank you to all the lovely folks and Beeston, Stapleford and Kimberley Libraries for cheering this book over the finishing line.

Thank you to Nellie, aka My Favourite Fluffy Co-Writer, for the cuddles, the purrs, the head-rubs and for keeping me company during all the late-night writing sessions.

And finally, huge thanks to you, for reading this book, for getting to the end, for even reading the acknowledgements. I hope that we can journey together again soon.

ABOUT THE AUTHOR

H L Schofield

H L Schofield lives in Nottingham with her family, alarmingly large book collection and frankly ridiculous cat. She works in a library. When not writing, she can be found running through forests, climbing up mountains, swimming in lakes, and generally being a feral little goblin creature.
Green Heart is her first novel.

Printed in Great Britain
by Amazon